"Col. David Giammona and Tr
battle cry to prepare. This inspi
cover your divine destiny and mission as the world watches events
unfold, leading to the glorious return of Jesus our Messiah."

Jonathan Bernis, CEO and president, Jewish Voice
Ministries International

"An incredibly relevant and timely book for the disorienting times in which we live. Mission, purpose, and calling, which are divinely guided and empowered, are essential to effectively serving God and others in the midst of chaos and uncertainty. David Giammona and Troy Anderson are uniquely qualified to guide us in exploring the deepest existential questions we face en route to discovering the unique mission and purpose God has for each of us. *Your Mission in God's Army* is an essential tool to achieve the apostle Paul's powerful resilience and mission focus—'I press on toward the goal for the prize of the upward call of God in Christ Jesus.'"

Major General Robert F. Dees, U.S. Army, retired;
president, National Center for Healthy Veterans;
author, The Resilience Trilogy

"Col. David J. Giammona and Troy Anderson present a compelling vision of God's army and what it means to be a true follower of Jesus Christ. Blending spiritual wisdom with real-world stories, this book calls every believer to wholeheartedly commit to their divine assignment. If you want to impact the world for the Kingdom, you need this book."

Jimmy Evans, founder, EndTimes.com;
author, *Tipping Point: The End Is Here*

"In a world filled with chaos, this book is a beacon of hope and direction. *Your Mission in God's Army* equips you with the tools to discover your unique role in God's plan. Col. David Giammona and Troy Anderson masterfully merge military strategy and biblical wisdom to empower believers for these crucial times."

Cynthia Garrett, TV host, author, producer, social activist,
political commentator, evangelist, and speaker

"*Your Mission in God's Army* pairs biblical wisdom with real-world experience. Too many Christians today unthinkingly adopt a worldly definition of success. Col. Giammona reorients your thinking, gives you clear action steps, and deepens your love for Christ in the process. Read this book. Be challenged. Be changed!"

Dr. Robert Jeffress, senior pastor, First Baptist Church, Dallas

"This book is a strategic masterpiece! Ronald Reagan said, 'Without God . . . there is no prompting of the conscience.' Men and women of conscience are called to this fight. *Your Mission in God's Army* is a timely and urgent battle cry for Christians to rise up with courage and purpose. Col. David Giammona and Troy Anderson are your guides to discerning your divine assignment and navigating the spiritual battlefield."

Chris Salcedo, TV host, NewsMax's *Chris Salcedo Show*

"I'm stoked about *Your Mission in God's Army* because it speaks to all of us about our role in these end times. I believe a book of this caliber and depth is needed today to strengthen and support those looking to discover their God-given purpose and assignment as biblical and world events unfold ever increasingly. Let's keep fighting the good fight, because we're at the tipping point. If there was ever a time to heed this call, it is now. A must-read!"

Kevin Sorbo, actor, *God's Not Dead* and *Left Behind: Rise of the Antichrist*

"David and Troy have put together an incredible manual to help Christians battle our way through cultural warfare. This book will equip you with the tools you need to thrive in these difficult days. Onward, Christian soldiers!"

Todd Starnes, bestselling author and journalist

YOUR
MISSION IN
GOD'S ARMY

Books by Col. David J. Giammona
and Troy Anderson

The Military Guide to Armageddon
The Military Guide to Disarming Deception
Your Mission in God's Army

YOUR MISSION IN GOD'S ARMY

DISCOVERING AND COMPLETING YOUR
FAITH-FILLED ASSIGNMENT
BEFORE CHRIST'S RETURN

★ ★ ★ ★

COL. DAVID J. GIAMMONA
AND TROY ANDERSON

Chosen

a division of Baker Publishing Group
Minneapolis, Minnesota

Published by Chosen Books
Minneapolis, Minnesota
ChosenBooks.com

Chosen Books is a division of
Baker Publishing Group, Grand Rapids, Michigan

Printed in the United States of America

ISBN 9780800763725 (paper)
ISBN 9780800763763 (casebound)
ISBN 9781493445073 (ebook)

Library of Congress Cataloging-in-Publication Control Number: 2023055043

Unless otherwise indicated, Scriptures taken from the Holy Bible, New International Version®, NIV®. Copyright © 1973, 1978, 1984, 2011 by Biblica, Inc.® Used by permission of Zondervan. All rights reserved worldwide. www.zondervan.com. The "NIV" and "New International Version" are trademarks registered in the United States Patent and Trademark Office by Biblica, Inc.®

Scripture quotations identified AMP are from the Amplified® Bible (AMP), copyright © 2015 by The Lockman Foundation. Used by permission. www.Lockman.org

Scripture quotations identified BLB are from the Berean Literal Bible © 2016 by Bible Hub and Berean Bible. Used by permission. All rights reserved.

Scripture quotations identified CEB are from the Common English Bible. © Copyright 2011 by the Common English Bible. All rights reserved. Used by permission.

Scripture quotations identified CEV are from the Contemporary English Version © 1991, 1992, 1995 by American Bible Society. Used by permission.

Scripture quotations identified ESV are from The Holy Bible, English Standard Version® (ESV®), copyright © 2001 by Crossway, a publishing ministry of Good News Publishers. Used by permission. All rights reserved. ESV Text Edition: 2016

Scripture quotations identified GNT are from the Good News Translation in Today's English Version-Second Edition. Copyright © 1992 by American Bible Society. Used by permission.

Scripture quotations identified KJV are from the King James Version of the Bible.

Scripture quotations identified MSG are taken from The Message, copyright © 1993, 2002, 2018 by Eugene H. Peterson. Used by permission of NavPress. All rights reserved. Represented by Tyndale House Publishers.

Scripture quotations identified NASB taken from the (NASB®) New American Standard Bible®, Copyright © 1960, 1971, 1977, 1995, 2020 by The Lockman Foundation. Used by permission. All rights reserved. www.lockman.org

Scripture quoted by permission. Quotations designated NET are from the NET Bible® copyright ©1996, 2019 by Biblical Studies Press, L.L.C. http://netbible.com. All rights reserved.

Scripture identified NKJV taken from the New King James Version®. Copyright © 1982 by Thomas Nelson. Used by permission. All rights reserved.

Scripture quotations identified NLT are taken from the Holy Bible, New Living Translation, copyright © 1996, 2004, 2015 by Tyndale House Foundation. Used by permission of Tyndale House Publishers, Carol Stream, Illinois 60188. All rights reserved.

The authors are represented by Alive Literary Agency, www.aliveliterary.com

24 25 26 27 28 29 30   7 6 5 4 3 2 1

I, Col. David Giammona, dedicate this book about our purpose and assignment to my seven grandchildren: Isaac, Michael, Eva, Faith, Luke, Xiomara and Luca. They are all awesome and their bright futures are ahead of them, each with a God-given path, talent and assignment. May God richly bless their lives for His glory.

★ ★ ★ ★

I, Troy Anderson, dedicate this book to the Holy Spirit, who has graciously guided me throughout my life into an amazing assignment in Adonai's Army. I also dedicate this book to my incredible wife, Irene, who, as we were writing *Your Mission in God's Army*, became ill with severe Covid pneumonia, severe sepsis, acute pancreatitis and other life-threatening conditions. A doctor told me she only had a fifty-fifty chance to live. Our Battle Ready Ministries team, along with our small group and friends, prayed for her fervently, and we believe the Lord miraculously saved her life. I further dedicate this book to our beautiful, intelligent and charming daughters, Marlee and Ashley. May you discover your God-given dreams in life and may the Lord richly bless you for His purposes.

CONTENTS

Part 4: Using Your Gifts

PREFACE

Why am I here? What is my purpose? What is the meaning of my life? Does God have a plan for me? Does He have a mission He wants me to fulfill? What is my assignment on earth? Do I have a destiny?

These are some of the ultimate questions many of us ask at different times in our lives. As we look around today's increasingly chaotic world, many are seeking answers to life's most perplexing questions amid these challenging times.

Today theologians and faith leaders say the world may be witnessing many of the signs that Jesus Christ said will signify His return to earth.

A 2020 Lifeway research poll found that nearly nine in ten pastors see at least some current events matching those Jesus said would occur shortly before He returns.[1] A 2022 Pew research poll found that 39 percent of American adults, including 63 percent of evangelical Christians, say they believe "we are living in the end times."[2]

As we speak at churches and conferences around the nation, one of the questions we are most often asked is "What is this life all about?" Along with that amazingly complex question is "Does God have an assignment for me in this world?"

My co-author, Troy Anderson, and I are often confronted with these kinds of questions in our travels and media exposure by individuals hungry for more than just the ordinary daily routines of living. With the myriad of distractions, life messes and multiplied stresses most of us encounter, it may be time for you to stop, pull away for a few minutes and contemplate the reason for your existence on earth.

This book, *Your Mission in God's Army: Discovering and Completing Your Faith-Filled Assignment before Christ's Return*, does just that. We will explore paths you may never thought of traveling, ways of looking at life decidedly different than before and tools provided to us through decades of experience in the military and journalism that will offer you insights that may have been kept from your field of vision until now.

So please sit back, relax and embark on a journey with us that will transform your life.

INTRODUCTION

Outstanding people have one thing in common: an absolute sense of mission.

Zig Ziglar, world-renowned author and speaker

The book you are holding, *Your Mission in God's Army*, will take you on a transformative journey to explore your life's purpose and assignment while answering some of life's most pervasive and difficult questions surrounding your existence on planet earth. We call them the four W's: Why am I here? What is my purpose? Who am I? And where am I going?

First we must explore what the majority consider their purpose, fulfillment in life and ultimate destiny. The best way to describe it is illustrated by an experience I had in the U.S. Army while talking with a fellow officer. He was relaying to me his plan for his career.

"First," he said, "I'm going to get promoted to captain; then, in about five or six years, promotion to major; after that, in another six or more years, I'll make it to lieutenant colonel; and

13

then I'll cap it off with promotion to full colonel and probably retire from service."

"That sounds great," I replied. "Then what?"

He retorted, "What do you mean?"

"Don't get me wrong. I think it's a wonderful plan, provided you actually get promoted to all those ranks. But what will you do after retirement?"

"I'll probably be a consultant of some sort."

"Great. Then what?"

With considerable annoyance, he replied, "Then I'll fully retire and enjoy life, probably travel, and do all the things I've always wanted to do."

"That's great. Then what?"

I could see his blood pressure beginning to rise. "Then I'll die!"

I went for the jugular. "Then what?"

"What do you mean, Chaplain? Death is the final destination!"

"No, it's not," I answered. "You just think it is. Actually, it's just the beginning of your eternal destiny."

That floored him.

It is not wrong to have a proposed plan for your life. *Proposed* because God will sometimes change your best-laid plans.

Most people view life through a narrow set of lenses focused only on this life and not our eternal destination. But consider the following Bible passage: "This is the promise which He Himself made to us: eternal life" (1 John 2:25 NASB). If we are to discover our purpose for the here and now, we must also discover the big picture—our ultimate destination. This passage in 1 John unlocks for us our real destiny and purpose: attaining eternal life.

Eternal life is not just ceaseless existence or unending life. The Bible tells us that eternal life is the abundant life we can live here and now as well as into eternity. According to the original Greek in that 1 John passage, "Eternal life, *aiōnios*, operates simultaneously *outside* of time, *inside* of time, and beyond time—i.e. what gives time its everlasting meaning for the believer through faith, yet is also time-independent."[1]

Eternal life does not focus on the future, then, but on the quality of the age it relates to. Thus believers live in eternal life right now, experiencing the quality of God's life as a present possession. This means that you can experience profuse and abundant life right now, no matter your circumstances, position, power, health, finances, status or anything else.

In John 7:37–38 Jesus expanded on eternal life:

> On the last and greatest day of the festival, Jesus stood and said in a loud voice, "Let anyone who is thirsty come to me and drink. Whoever believes in me, as Scripture has said, rivers of living water will flow from within them."

Here, then, is the foundational principle and purpose for your life: At the very core of your being, you can have the life of Jesus Christ, the power of the Holy Spirit and the communion of the Father.

If you have committed your life to Christ, rivers of joy, peace and power should be flowing out of your being. If you are not experiencing the gushing joy, presence and flow of the Holy Spirit in your life, it is time for repentance, restoration, reexamination and renewal. We will be exploring these in depth in this book.

At the very core of our purpose is the central figure of Jesus Christ. Without Him there is no purpose or future or even life itself, because He is the center of all things, and all things were created for Him, not us:

> The Son is the image of the invisible God, the firstborn over all creation. For in him all things were created: things in heaven

and on earth, visible and invisible, whether thrones or powers or rulers or authorities; all things have been created through him and for him.

Colossians 1:15–16

Polls tells us that most Americans are unhappy with their jobs, lives, mates and financial status. According to one news headline in 2022: *Job unhappiness is at a staggering all-time high, according to Gallup.*[2] Everyone is looking for love, as the title of a country hit recorded by Johnny Lee says, "in all the wrong places."

Whether in relationships, careers, finances, sports, video-games, TV, movies, apps or any other number of pursuits, satisfaction usually drops off sharply not long after people acquire what they were pursuing. That is why many are frustrated and want to know their true purpose in life. Even those who attend church often ask themselves this question.

To help you gain a new sense of purpose and direction in these difficult days, we will start by investigating how the military assigns those who join its ranks. Then we will explore how Old and New Testament followers of God—the great biblical heroes of old—were chosen and how they fulfilled their callings. We will learn how followers of Christ hear and understand their present-day callings. We will understand why today's pervasive philosophies of humanism and modernism lead people astray. We will see how not to be afraid of the Lord's direction and calling. And we will explore how we can lead a fulfilling, exciting, light-filled journey as He leads us in paths of victory.

During these tumultuous and quickly changing times, you will learn who the Commander of the heavenly armies is; how He operates in unlimited power and wisdom; how His plan is unfolding for you; and how you can join His team. You will learn how the military processes assignments that parallel our biblical assignments; how to grow in your assignment; and how to be a great follower *and* a great leader.

At the end of each chapter, we will include strategic spiritual exercises that will provide practical suggestions to help you find your purpose and assignment in life.

Let's get started on a few right now.

Strategic Spiritual Exercises

1. Take some time now to look at your current purpose and assignment. Compare each to 1 John 2:25. Do they correspond or fall short?

2. As you embark on this journey, identify someone you trust to look with you at your life, and connect with him or her.

3. Look through the following Scriptures methodically, prayerfully and meditatively: John 6:68; John 17:3; Titus 1:2; and 2 Peter 1:11. Can you identify with each of these? If not, why not?

4. On a scale of one to ten, how satisfied are you right now with your life?

5. Take a moment to pray and ask the Lord to reveal His mission for you as you read this book.

PART 1

THE MISSION

1

WHAT IS YOUR ASSIGNMENT?

We are God's masterpiece. He has created us anew in Christ Jesus, so we can do the good things he planned for us long ago.

Ephesians 2:10 NLT

Summer 2008. Presidential Tower, 12th floor, Crystal City, Virginia. Early morning. My new boss greets me with, "Welcome to the office of the chief of chaplains, Chaplain Giammona. You are now the 'subject matter expert' involving personnel assignments for all our chaplains."

I thought about that for a moment and replied, "Thank you, sir. I appreciate the opportunity to serve here, but I hardly think I am an SME, having just started this job today."

His reply was priceless: "It doesn't matter. You are now the go-to guy for all our seventeen hundred chaplains worldwide, whether you know the answers or not. It's your job! By the way, I need nine chaplains assigned immediately to go to war."

I was off to the races.

Sometime later I sat down to think about how I got this important assignment. I did not ask for it. In fact, I was hoping for another Army chaplain job that had me closer to the troops instead of administration. Through a series of events, I found myself working for the then chief of chaplains, Douglas Carver, as his assignment officer. It was the exact job I needed at the time. I was able, with the help of God and my chaplain managers, to influence the lives of hundreds of Army chaplains and their families.

The Army is always looking for a few good people to bring into the force, whether it is full time (active duty) or in the reserves (one weekend a month). They have a process to make that determination. Not everyone is qualified or fit to endure the rigors of the military lifestyle. The criteria involve mental and physical fitness, attitude, drive to excel and many other benchmarks. They discriminate! They do not take everybody. That is why only one percent of the American population serves in the military.

In the same manner, God is looking for those few who will seek Him diligently. Second Chronicles 16:9 says, "The eyes of the LORD range throughout the earth to strengthen those whose hearts are fully committed to him." Jesus said, "Wide is the gate and broad is the road that leads to destruction, and many enter through it. But small is the gate and narrow the road that leads to life, and only a few find it" (Matthew 7:13–14). It is time for all of us to seek God and set our priorities to do the assignment He has tasked us with. No other path works for followers of Christ.

But if we are to know and understand our mission and assignment here on planet earth, we must first define the words.

The word *mission*, according to the *Cambridge Dictionary*, means "an important job, especially a military one, that someone is sent somewhere to do: Your mission is to isolate the enemy by destroying all the bridges across the river." *Mission* is also defined as "any work that someone believes it is their duty to do."[1] To be "on assignment," according to the *Cambridge Dictionary*, is "doing a particular job or piece of work, usually in a particular place where they have been sent for a period of time."[2]

Now let's look at the biblical definition of *mission*. According to the *Evangelical Dictionary of Biblical Theology*:

> Mission is the divine activity of sending intermediaries, whether supernatural or human, to speak or do God's will so that his purposes for judgment or redemption are furthered. . . . The biblical concept of "mission" comprehends the authority of the one who sends; the obedience of the one sent; a task to be accomplished; the power to accomplish the task; and a purpose within the moral framework of God's covenantal working of judgment or redemption.[3]

God Created You for a Purpose!

Each one of us has an assignment in this life given to us by God. Not only is He the One who sends us the assignment (as in the definition just above), but He gives us the power to accomplish it. What we must do is be willing to listen to our Commander-in-Chief, obey His instructions and walk worthy of His calling.

The fact is, God has many assignments for our lives, which come at different times and places, under unforeseen circumstances or through people placed in our lives at just the right time. A Bible verse may speak to you, or maybe something a pastor says. They could come from someone you know or someone you do not know—or from someone as near as your spouse, child or friend.

Because here is the thing: You are not some haphazard mistake who just happened to be born. Evolutionists will tell you that you are an accident in a purposeless universe according to random chance—but the following Scriptures indicate clearly that God created you and me for a purpose:

> "I have raised you up for this very purpose, that I might show you my power and that my name might be proclaimed in all the earth."
>
> Exodus 9:16

> "I know that you [God] can do all things; no purpose of yours can be thwarted."
>
> Job 42:2

> The LORD has made everything for its own purpose, even the wicked for the day of evil.
>
> Proverbs 16:4 NASB

> Many are the plans in a person's heart, but it is the LORD's purpose that prevails.
>
> Proverbs 19:21

The life of Jesus is our prime example of how God works in our lives. At the very beginning of His ministry, He read His mission statement to the crowd in the synagogue in his hometown of Nazareth, out of the scroll of Isaiah:

> "The Spirit of the Lord is upon me, because he has anointed me to proclaim good news to the poor. He has sent me to proclaim liberty to the captives and recovering of sight to the blind, to set at liberty those who are oppressed, to proclaim the year of the Lord's favor."
>
> Luke 4:18–19 ESV

This was Jesus' assignment from the Father from which He did not deviate. When He read His mission to the people of His town that day, it caused such a stir that they tried to throw Him off the cliff. God's assignment to His Son was not an easy one. No one says God's plans are easy. Just ask Moses, David, Joshua, Gideon, Jonah and the rest.

While your assignment may not be easy, it is full of divine purpose, promise and power. In fact, there is no better way to live life than to live it according to God's plan. All you must do is stay the course.

From day one Jesus stayed the course set by His Father. This little story helps us understand the focus Jesus had from the Father:

> Someone from the crowd said to him, "Teacher, tell my brother to divide the inheritance with me." But Jesus said to him, "Man, who made me a judge or arbitrator between you two?" Then he said to them, "Watch out and guard yourself from all types of greed, because one's life does not consist in the abundance of his possessions."
>
> Luke 12:13–15 NET

It is easy to get sidetracked by many important things from our main task as followers of Christ. And here, coming to Jesus, was a man with some important financial issues who wanted his share of the inheritance. He saw that Jesus was a righteous man, one he could trust, so why not ask Him to investigate this matter? But Jesus knew His mission from the Father, and that mission was to bring salvation to mankind through His death on the cross and subsequent resurrection.

In case you are wondering if this has anything to do with you, it does. You may be saying, "I don't plan on going into missionary work, or becoming a minister or doing anything related to full-time ministry, so the concept of 'mission' doesn't really relate to me."

Fact: Missions and assignments from God are neither sacred nor secular. We will explore this more in chapter 3. The psalmist wrote: "I say to the LORD, 'You are my Lord; apart from you I have no good thing'" (Psalm 16:2). In God's view there are no distinctions between sacred and secular, the eternal and the temporal. He owns it all. It does not matter if you are going down the path to become a doctor, engineer, rocket scientist, real estate salesman or movie star. All truth is God's truth and all assignments for followers of Christ come from Him. He can and will use the talents He has given you for His purpose, if you let Him.

Learning from Failure

Kevin Sorbo, one of Hollywood's top stars who rose to fame in the 1990s, decided to become an actor at age eleven when he went to see a Shakespeare play at a famous theater in his hometown of Minneapolis. He recounts:

> I didn't know what the heck they were saying, because I was eleven years old and it was Shakespeare. But I remember being mesmerized by the actors onstage, and I made up my mind, telling my parents, that I would be an actor. I didn't start pursuing it until I got into college, but I started watching a lot of old Hollywood movies with Humphrey Bogart and Spencer Tracy and Jimmy Stewart and those guys. I love that old style. I love how original Hollywood was back then. I wanted to get involved in movies that had more of a positive influence on people.[4]

Sorbo got his big break in Hollywood with *Hercules: The Legendary Journeys*, which began as a series of television movies and later became one of the highest-rated syndicated TV shows in the world. He says:

> Universal Studios loved it, made it a series by our third movie, and it became the most watched show in the world, seen in 176 countries. I had nothing to do with the writing of the storylines, although I wrote one episode, but I got to give the writers input. Even though it was mythological, they put good moral messages in there. They made me a very righteous guy and they put a lot of humor in it, too, which I thought was important.
>
> Hollywood wouldn't make a show like that today. But there are eighty million homes out there that want the kind of movies I do—and a lot of people in Hollywood in power positions who are afraid to speak out. It's like a clique in high school where you'd better be hanging with the "right" guys, and people are afraid to speak out.
>
> In pretty much every movie I do, I get one or two people coming up and saying, "Hey, I love what you're doing. Thanks for being a voice for us."[5]

Some Christians in Hollywood get blacklisted for being vocal about their faith, but Sorbo says his career has taken off making primarily faith-based films—films like *God's Not Dead*, *Soul Surfer* and *Left Behind: Rise of the Antichrist*. He has developed a solid base of fans, he says, and knows many in the entertainment industry. Sorbo says:

> I've been shooting four or five movies a year for the last eleven years after Hollywood gave me the boot, so I've been very fortunate to keep busy. But I want people to have a voice, and not let Hollywood and the mainstream media and the cancel-culture world put fear in them, because fear is the greatest weapon of our government. They love fear, and they love controlling us with fear—but we have to stop being afraid. The only person we need to fear is God.[6]

27

As the fourth of five children, although the family had little money, Sorbo learned from his dad, a public school teacher, the importance of patience, persistence and perseverance. He remembers:

> We had parents who pushed us, parents who believed in hard work, parents who believed in not expecting handouts, parents who supported the decisions we made. All five of us kids took a completely different road in life, but each of us had success in whatever we did. So I tell people all the time, failure is a good thing.
>
> I learned that very quickly from wealthy people I used to caddy for when I was in college. I worked at a private country club carrying two golf bags, 36 holes a day, and I would ask those guys, "How did you become successful?" They all said the same thing: "I failed and then I failed again. Oh, and by the way, I failed and failed and failed." That motivated me!
>
> Look, I'm a thirty-year "overnight" success in Hollywood. I've had plenty of doors slammed in my face, but all that did was motivate me. Failure can be a good thing. It teaches you a lot, because you can take the bits of good stuff out of every failure, and get rid of the other stuff, and keep growing and make yourself a better and stronger person.[7]

Given his experiences in Hollywood and success in the entertainment industry, Sorbo offers this advice for discovering and completing your God-given assignment:

> We all have a purpose in life, and I think people put too much pressure on themselves to find out whatever that purpose is. I tell people all the time, "You had a dream at one time and now you've lost that dream because you gave up so quickly."[8]

Again, stay the course.

Lessons from Jesus

We do not know exactly when Jesus received His mission from His Father, but we do know that at the age of twelve, he already had profound knowledge of the Scriptures and His Father's house. Recall the time, following the Passover feast in Jerusalem, that His parents headed back home to Nazareth, thinking He was with the caravan of their friends and relatives—but He was not.

> When they did not find Him, they returned to Jerusalem, looking for Him. Then, after three days they found Him in the temple, sitting in the midst of the teachers, both listening to them and asking them questions. And all who heard Him were amazed at His understanding and His answers.
>
> When Joseph and Mary saw Him, they were bewildered; and His mother said to Him, "Son, why have You treated us this way? Behold, Your father and I have been anxiously looking for You!" And He said to them, "Why is it that you were looking for Me? Did you not know that I had to be in My Father's house?" And yet they on their part did not understand the statement which He had made to them.
>
> And He went down with them and came to Nazareth, and He continued to be subject to them; and His mother treasured all these things in her heart.
>
> Luke 2:45–51 NASB

At least three key points in this story help us with our own mission and assignments in life.

1. Timing

The first point is preparation. The Bible says that, immediately following this incident, Jesus "grew in wisdom and stature, and in favor with God and man" (Luke 2:52). That is a powerful statement! Jesus, who was God in the flesh, had to grow up and mature in His understanding of God, the Scriptures, His relationships, even His physical body, and He did not arrive all at once. It took time. In fact, it took Jesus eighteen more years from the age of twelve (the start of manhood for the Jews) to age thirty, when He started His mission and assignment. During that time He was increasing in all aspects of maturity. He was preparing.

Assignments from God take time. Time is needed for spiritual maturity, for learning, for building relationships, for gaining work experience and for learning from our failures. It takes an average of seven to ten years of preparation, for example, for a chaplain to be accessioned onto active duty in the Army.

Don't be afraid to take time for preparation. It is ordained by God. Enjoy the journey and the process, not just the final destination.

Moses was given an assignment by God at the burning bush. He had been tending sheep in the wilderness for forty years and then, in a single day, everything changed. God had chosen him for a particular task—to deliver the Israelites out of slavery in Egypt and bring them into the Promised Land.

Because Moses had been raised up in Pharaoh's household, he knew the royal culture, the way things ran, the ins and outs of the Egyptian hierarchy. Then God sent Moses to the school of hard knocks, tending sheep in the desert for forty years. But when he was ready, God called him.

2. Listening

The second point we learn from the story of Jesus being found in the Temple by His parents involves the importance of listening—especially listening to others, to those you trust and to those who may have traveled the path before you.

This is an important part of the assignment process in the Army. As an assignments officer, I had to listen to my superiors, my peers, and those to whom I was making an assignment. I had to get it right for everyone's sake, including the families of those whose lives would be affected.

Notice that Jesus' parents "found Him in the temple, sitting in the midst of the teachers, both *listening* to them and asking them questions" (Luke 2:46, emphasis added). Here was Jesus, the Lord of all creation, listening to the senior rabbis in the Temple.

In our own culture, we have lost the art of listening—of sitting with people and hearing not only what they are saying but observing their body language, their demeanor, their emotions and their hearts. Jesus does that for us. Do we do that for others?

As I studied for my master's degree, I learned that the art of listening is one of the most important things in becoming a counselor and therapist. It is emphasized over and over. Listening involves an attitude and posture of the heart, mind, body and soul. The greatest and most respected leaders are the ones who have learned the art and skills of listening. Undoubtedly the greatest listener in history is Jesus Christ.

3. Obeying

A third and final point we learn from Jesus in the Temple story is obedience. Notice that, after His parents found Him, Jesus "went down with them and came to Nazareth, and He continued to be subject to them" (Luke 2:51 NASB).

Yes, His parents were angry and worried about Him. They had been searching for Him in Jerusalem for three days. Can you imagine all the things they were thinking and going through to find their lost son? When they found Him, He did not put up an argument. He could have said, "This is My Father's house, and I am staying here to do the work My Father has given me to do." But it was not time yet, so He simply subjected himself in obedience to His parents.

The Bible tells us that "when the fullness of the time had come, God sent forth His Son" (Galatians 4:4 NKJV). That Jesus appeared in "the fullness of time" means that when the time was right, it happened.

There is a saying often quoted in the Army: "To be a great leader, you must be a great follower." There is tremendous truth in this saying. Jesus lived this out by subjecting Himself to His parents, for they had been given authority over Him by God.

An old hymn tells us to "trust and obey, for there is no other way to be happy in Jesus, but to trust and obey."[9] Hebrews 11:6 tells us that God "is a rewarder of those who diligently seek Him" (NKJV). If we truly are followers of Christ, we must learn not only to listen but to obey His leading, guidance and commands.

One final important note about your assignment, purpose and mission. You may ask, "Is my assignment my work, calling, vocation, marriage, parenting, church or ministry?" The answer is yes. More to follow in the next chapter.

Strategic Spiritual Exercises

1. Start a journal of your new adventure with God. Write in it every day the things God is speaking to your heart, especially as they relate to your assignment and mission. You will be surprised by how much He is speaking, directing and moving in your life.

2. Get alone with God tonight or tomorrow, review all the Scriptures in this chapter, and begin to assess your priorities. If you do not yet know your assignment, begin to inquire of the Lord according to Psalm 53:2, Jeremiah 29:13 and Isaiah 55:6.

3. Practice the art of listening by focusing on what God, your spouse, your close friends and your relatives have been saying to you. Don't plan your responses, but center your attention fully on their dialogue. Jot down what you hear.

4. Visualize an encounter with Jesus walking into your room while you are praying and speaking to you about what He wants you to do. What do you notice? What is He saying? What is your response?

2

PREPARING FOR YOUR MISSION

"Which of you, desiring to build a tower, does not first, having sat down, count the cost, whether he has enough for its completion?"

Luke 14:28 BLB

Early 2003. Operations hangar, Campbell Army Airfield, Fort Campbell, Kentucky. Preparing to deploy to Operation Iraqi Freedom. "You are deploying to war in Iraq with the 101st Airborne Division, is that right?" I asked the journalist.

"That's correct, Chaplain," replied the journalist. "We're here to cover the war embedded in these combat infantry units."

"How much training did you go through with these guys?"

"None."

"Let me get this straight. You are about to go into harm's way with one of the most elite and lethal combat units in the world with no training? Son, do you not understand that the next plane you get on may be in a body bag?"

That journalist failed to realize that without the right training, he was possibly going to end up getting killed or getting someone else killed defending him. He probably thought he would be okay since he would be surrounded by professional soldiers who would protect him. The truth is that in war, as well as in life, going into combat requires time, training, rigorous preparation . . . and prayer.

In 1944 General George S. Patton, one of the greatest generals in American history, directed his chaplain, Monsignor James H. O'Neill, to write a training letter on his behalf to all the Third Army soldiers concerning prayer. It read, in part:

> Urge all of your men to pray, not alone in church, but everywhere. Pray when driving. Pray when fighting. Pray alone. Pray with others. Pray by night and pray by day. Pray for the cessation of immoderate rains, for good weather for Battle. Pray for the defeat of our wicked enemy whose banner is injustice and whose good is oppression. Pray for victory. Pray for our Army, and pray for Peace. We must march together, all out for God.[1]

Before anyone starts a great project, much time, planning, strategy and financial considerations must be invested, or that project will fail. Countless examples of those who jump into ventures without due diligence are strewn all over our land. According to small business failure statistics, only about twenty percent of "new businesses survive past their first year of operation. Around half of all businesses no longer exist after five years. Only one-third make it past their tenth anniversary."[2]

Many people want to jump right into relationships, assignments, life's work, ministries or callings without the requisite spiritual, mental, emotional and sometimes physical preparation necessary to accomplish the task God has ordained. Many young adults want to achieve the same level of income and status as their parents without going through all the steps required to get there. There are no shortcuts in life. That is why lottery winners, professional sports figures and celebrities often end up broke; they lack the discipline, training, guidance, education or understanding of how to handle money.

Just as the military goes to great lengths to prepare soldiers for combat, God is in the business of preparing us for our assignments here and now—and for eternity as well. Years ago I told a friend in college, "God will use this time in school to prepare you for your mission in life." But he dropped out because he felt the coming of the Lord was at hand.

Todd Smith, leader of the North Georgia Revival and senior pastor of Christ Fellowship Church in Dawsonville, Georgia, says that finding your assignment comes from the realization that you do have an assignment and from relinquishment to God's purpose. He explains:

> It is in dying, in yielding, in surrender, and in the submission of my total will to be encapsulated by the will of the Father for me—losing my life to the point that I say, "God, I have no agenda but Yours, no goal but Yours"—that the full revelation of His purpose for my life can be realized. Not only identified but realized. It is in the losing, in the releasing of my dreams and aspirations, that I fully find out what He wants me to do. His gifting will be there; His anointing will accompany me.
>
> But there can't be a mixture. There must be a complete surrender, presenting our bodies as a living sacrifice. First Corinthians 9:27 says for me to make my body a slave of His—an instrument, according to Romans 6:13, of righteousness. So that is my advice. It is in utter yieldedness and brokenness that I fully discover His plan and purpose for me.[3]

Joseph's Rigorous Preparation

One of the great preparation stories in the Bible is the life of Joseph. Before he could become a ruler in Egypt and save his people during a time of extended famine, he had to undergo rigorous preparation, painful life circumstances, unfair treatment and the hatred of his brothers. His story in the Bible communicates to us some important life lessons about preparation. The story starts in Genesis 37:2–8:

> Joseph, a young man of seventeen, was tending the flocks with his brothers . . . and he brought their father a bad report about them.
>
> Now Israel loved Joseph more than any of his other sons, because he had been born to him in his old age; and he made an ornate robe for him. When his brothers saw that their father loved him more than any of them, they hated him and could not speak a kind word to him.
>
> Joseph had a dream, and when he told it to his brothers, they hated him all the more. He said to them, "Listen to this dream I had: We were binding sheaves of grain out in the field when suddenly my sheaf rose and stood upright, while your sheaves gathered around mine and bowed down to it."
>
> His brothers said to him, "Do you intend to reign over us? Will you actually rule us?" And they hated him all the more because of his dream and what he had said.

Joseph had a second similar dream—with no idea that he would be sold into slavery, accused of rape and then thrown into prison for years, before ascending to the position of second in command of all of Egypt. One of the key principles we notice, then, is that a dream does not necessarily mean the event is going to happen immediately; some dreams, like Joseph's, take years to accomplish.

Another key principle in this story is humility. Life can be like sandpaper that keeps rubbing off the rough edges of our lives. As a teenager, Joseph unwisely flaunted his dreams in front of his father and brothers. After years of trials and difficulties, he learned that promotion is from God, and he learned humility through what he suffered.

In the New Testament, we find that the Son of God also learned obedience in this way:

> In the days of his flesh, Jesus offered up prayers and supplications, with loud cries and tears, to him who was able to save him from death, and he was heard because of his reverence. Although he was a son, he learned obedience through what he suffered. And being made perfect, he became the source of eternal salvation to all who obey him, being designated by God a high priest after the order of Melchizedek.
>
> Hebrews 5:7–10 ESV

Suffering is out of vogue, especially in Western culture. But we learn more about ourselves through suffering than when things are going well. It is part of the preparation process, and God can use it to bless others.

Richard Wurmbrand, founder of Voice of the Martyrs, suffered daily for fourteen years in the Communist prisons of Romania. But later he turned his suffering to ministry for the masses undergoing persecution around the world. He wrote in his book *Tortured for Christ*:

> You free Christians are part of the same Body of Christ that is now beaten in prisons in restricted nations, that even now gives martyrs for Christ. Can you not feel our pain? The Early Church in all of its beauty, sacrifice, and dedication has come alive again in these countries.[4]

A third principle in the life of Joseph is perseverance. Imagine Joseph stuck in prison for all those years, yet he persevered and saw it through to the end. So don't give up; make small investments in your dream daily and allow God to prepare you.

The Bible tells us not to despise "the day of small things (beginnings)" (Zechariah 4:10 AMP). Small beginnings are slow, often difficult, sometimes lonely and with no end in sight. That is why many give up on the dreams God has given them. But if you continue, seek counsel, gather peers and wise people, and pray continually, you will see God's purposes come to fruition.

Todd Smith of the North Georgia Revival empathizes with Joseph and the suffering he endured, noting that the process of drawing close to God, discovering one's mission in God's army, and learning to walk in the supernatural power, protection and provision of the Holy Spirit involves a "perpetual state of death":

> I know that's unpopular, but it's dying to myself. And it is very hard to stay dead because my flesh wants to be resurrected. All that is in the world is the lust of the eyes, lust of the flesh, and the pride of life. I deal with that constantly—all of us do. It is that continuous state of suppression that I am beating my body daily, as the Word says, literally into submission—a battle we fight every single day.
>
> I discovered this when I asked the Lord, "God, increase Your glory in my life. Increase the manifestation of Your power in our church." I heard the Spirit of the Lord speak to me as clearly as I hear your voice. He said, "Then increase your brokenness."
>
> It's an inversion. The more broken I am, the more weight of God I can carry. The more yielded I am, the stronger I become. The church world has been about self-preservation, about my agenda, my goal, my destiny. It's hard to convince our minds of this, but it's in dying that I live; it's in yielding that I thrive. This turns the church world upside down.[5]

With the speed of life accelerating and the promised Second Coming of Christ on the horizon, many want to bypass the critical time of training and jump unwisely right into their assignments. This can have disastrous effects—like discouragement, falling into sin and a host of other debilitating consequences.

Matthew 24:42 tells us that we are to watch for signs of Jesus' impending return. But we cannot know when this will be. Mark 13:32 says, "About that day or hour no one knows, not even the angels in heaven, nor the Son, but only the Father." This is why it is important that, although we see signs of Christ's return—and polls show that most faith leaders and believers view current events as signals of Christ's impending return[6]—we recognize that we do not know the "day or hour." So we should be allowing God to prepare us day by day to complete the assignments He has given each of us. As Jesus said:

> "Who then is the faithful and wise servant, whom the master has put in charge of the servants in his household to give them their food at the proper time? It will be good for that servant whose master finds him doing so when he returns. Truly I tell you, he will put him in charge of all his possessions."
>
> Matthew 24:45–47

At the end of his journey, Joseph, "the faithful and wise servant," found his dreams fulfilled. He ruled in Egypt, second only to Pharaoh, and enabled his Jewish brothers and sisters to survive the severe famine. As Joseph looked back on the events of his life, he declared to the very brothers who sold him into slavery: "You intended to harm me, but God intended it for good to accomplish what is now being done, the saving of many lives" (Genesis 50:20).

41

Starting from Faith

The reason this book mentions in its subtitle *Your Faith-Filled Assignment* is that, if we are to please God, we must do everything in this life by faith. If we think for a single moment that we are in control of our own future, we are living in denial. The Bible clearly indicates that it is God who has the power and purpose: "Many are the plans in a person's heart, but it is the LORD's purpose that prevails" (Proverbs 19:21). Job 12:10 says, "It is God who directs the lives of his creatures; everyone's life is in his power" (GNT). And "Everything got started in him and finds its purpose in [God's Son]" (Colossians 1:16 MSG). We must place our very lives into His divine hands and plans.

Colossians 1 goes on to explain that we were created by God for His purpose and that our lives are part of His larger cosmic plan:

> [Christ] was there before [anything] came into existence and holds it all together right up to this moment. And when it comes to the church, he organizes and holds it together, like a head does a body.
>
> He was supreme in the beginning and—leading the resurrection parade—he is supreme in the end. From beginning to end he's there, towering far above everything, everyone. So spacious is he, so expansive, that everything of God finds its proper place in him without crowding. Not only that, but all the broken and dislocated pieces of the universe—people and things, animals and atoms—get properly fixed and fit together in vibrant harmonies, all because of his death, his blood that poured down from the cross.
>
> Colossians 1:17–20 MSG

Make no mistake about it, however: Even though God directs our lives, we have free will and have a big part to play in developing our God-given talents into the stuff of reality. It is God who breathes life into us at the moment of conception, and it is He who will guide us. But we must allow the Holy Spirit to lead us into all that He has planned for us.

A great example of this is found in the life of world-class soccer player Lionel Messi of Argentina. He says:

> The truth is I didn't do anything, it was God who made me play like this. Obviously he gave me that gift, I have no doubt about that. He chose me and, obviously, I then did everything possible to try to improve myself and achieve success. But obviously, without His help, I would not have gotten anywhere.[7]

It is a common error on the part of parents to tell their children that they can become anything they want. The truth is, parents, along with teachers and mentors, must help children discover what God-given abilities, drives, passions and desires lie within them. This is no easy task, but it is necessary to achieve all that God has for them. It is a team effort. We must train our young people to "do it all for the glory of God" (1 Corinthians 10:31).

I have a passion for the saxophone. Growing up, I would practice innumerable hours. No one had to force me to practice. I had the God-given drive to do it. I did not really begin to excel, however, until my parents hired a private tutor while I was in high school. Then I went on to California State University, Sacramento, to hone my skills in their great music department. God had given me the passion and drive, and then my skills were developed by more experienced teachers and professors. I have used these skills under God's divine direction in countless concerts, churches and venues around the world.

Let's look at the word *faith* and how it plays an essential role in terms of our assignment, and a key role in just about everything in life:

> Faith is confidence in what we hope for and assurance about what we do not see. This is what the ancients were commended for. By faith we understand that the universe was formed at God's command, so that what is seen was not made out of what was visible. . . . Without faith it is impossible to please God, because anyone who comes to him must believe that he exists and that he rewards those who earnestly seek him.
>
> Hebrews 11:1–3, 6

What is faith, why is it so important and how can it shape your mission and assignment? Simply put, faith is putting our trust in what God says in His Word. If He said it, we can and must believe it. According to the late Adrian Rogers, founder of Love Worth Finding Ministries, "Don't put faith in faith, put faith in Jesus."[8]

Here are powerful verses to memorize:

> If you declare with your mouth, "Jesus is Lord," and believe in your heart that God raised him from the dead, you will be saved. For it is with your heart that you believe and are justified, and it is with your mouth that you profess your faith and are saved.
>
> Romans 10:9–10

You are saved by believing in your heart that God sent Jesus to die for you, and then speaking that belief with your mouth, declaring that Jesus is Lord. Notice that you are not saved by mere consent to an idea or making a formal nod to God. No, you are saved by genuine faith in the living Christ, thereby establishing an eternal relationship with Him.

And that is just the beginning. Your faith must be nurtured by pastors and spiritually mature individuals—trained, grown and manifested throughout your life. It is part of preparing for your mission.

So take that same faith and apply it to your assignment in life. It comes out of what God has placed in your heart and is nurtured by speaking and activating those gifts, talents, abilities, drive and desires that God Himself has placed there. These are confirmed along your journey by parents, teachers, coaches, trainers, pastors, mentors and others whom God uses.

Your mission does not have to be a so-called "sacred" vocation, as we will see in the next chapter. You have a call of God on your life, period!

=== STRATEGIC SPIRITUAL EXERCISES ===

1. What has God placed in your heart and life as His assignment? What Scriptures has He used to speak to you? Who is God placing in your life to help you?

2. Consider your prayer life. What are one or two ways you can expand your life of prayer?

3. Study the life of Moses and Joseph from the discussion in this chapter and note similarities you find between their lives and yours. In what ways do they challenge you?

4. Are there people who have achieved great things in the areas you are drawn to? What did they do? How did they do it? Choose at least one biography and read it.

3

SACRED VS. SECULAR

There is not a square inch in the whole domain of our human existence over which Christ, who is Sovereign over all, does not cry: "Mine!"

Abraham Kuyper, prime minister
of the Netherlands, 1901–1905

Mid-1980s. Sixth Army Headquarters, the Presidio, San Francisco. Phone call with a U.S. Army chaplain recruiter. "The best thing about the Army chaplaincy," stated the recruiter, "is that you go wherever your troops go, do whatever your troops do, and best of all, you are one of the troops. The troops see you as one of their own, so there is no difference between you and them."

I was astounded that God was opening a door for me that would shape the next three decades of my life and beyond.

I had heard the call of God earlier that week at a Marine Corps graduation ceremony at Camp Pendleton. I knew God was speaking, but I had no idea what would come next. So I took the next logical step and went to the local recruiter.

He asked me about my educational background and what I was interested in doing in the Army. I told him I had a degree in music and was a licensed minister with the Assemblies of God. After a few minutes talking about music, he asked me if I was interested in becoming a chaplain.

"What's a chaplain?" I asked.

"A chaplain is a minister to the military," he replied. Then he gave me the number of the chaplain recruiter.

The rest, as they say, is history.

As I look back at the many years I spent training in the field with the troops, doing physical training (PT) early every morning, spending time with them in the most miserable conditions, going to war with them, and being at their side when they were injured or dying, I would not trade one minute for all the gold in the world. You see, when God calls you into a particular area of endeavor, He will make a way, sustain you and grant you the grace to fulfill your destiny; plus He will grant you His peace, blessing and strength.

What I loved about being a chaplain was that there was no dividing line between sacred and secular. To me and the soldiers around me, everything was sacred. Religious services, whether in combat, training or some field exercise, were held anytime and anywhere, whether from the hood of a Humvee, under a clump of trees or in an underground bunker. It did not matter because every day was a holy day. And it did not matter to most of the soldiers, regardless of their denominational preference or religious background; they wanted to participate in something sacred before laying their lives on the line.

Living by Faith

We have already seen that every follower of Christ has a destiny planned by God—in this life and in the next life with Him in heaven. You have a call of God on your life, period! You may say, "I'm not called into ministry." But we are all called by God to fulfill an eternal purpose on planet earth.

It is important for us to avoid the trap of dividing our lives between "sacred" and "secular." In fact, in Christ there is no sacred versus secular: He owns it all. There is no difference between the so-called "sacred" vocations of chaplain or missionary and the so-called "secular" vocations of selling life insurance or becoming a doctor. All of them are sacred vocations and assignments if God has led you into them.

There are things people do that are inherently sinful—not only being a terrorist or thief or murderer but engaging in dishonest business dealings or turning a blind eye to a neighbor in need. God is the sovereign Lord of the universe, and nothing goes unnoticed by Him. In the end we will all stand before Him to give an account of our lives, whether it is in the Great White Throne Judgment for sinners (see Revelation 20:11–12) or before the Judgment Seat of Christ for believers (see 2 Corinthians 5:10).

Many people today live one way at work, another way at home and still another at church. They claim their faith is a private affair and not shared or shown to others. Some political leaders do not allow their faith to inform their views or policies. So in this chapter we explore opposites: sacred and secular, faith and unbelief.

Some claim that the opposite of faith is reason. Not true! Faith and reason can coexist side by side.

We saw in the last chapter that faith is putting our trust in what God says in His Word and living according to it. The *Cambridge Dictionary* defines *reason* as "the ability of a healthy mind to think and make judgments, especially based on practical facts."[1] Remember that it is God who gives mankind the ability to think and make sound judgments. Where many get turned around is the idea that we need only reason. They say, "We don't need God or faith. We are superior human beings who evolved from nothing into these marvelous thinking machines." This type of reasoning is called unbelief. It is why many evolutionists hold tightly to their theory—because if we did not evolve, then there must be an intelligent Designer behind the intelligent design of the universe.

But many today have chosen reason to rule their lives, purpose and assignments in life. Reason is enthroned by fallen mankind as the god of the universe. Science, reason, technology and education are the foundations of life where many find their center. But the Bible says:

> Do not love the world or anything in the world. If anyone loves the world, love for the Father is not in them. For everything in the world—the lust of the flesh, the lust of the eyes, and the pride of life—comes not from the Father but from the world. The world and its desires pass away, but whoever does the will of God lives forever.
>
> 1 John 2:15–17

There are many ways people living according to the world's system choose to plan out their lives. They are influenced by economic conditions, media personalities, sports figures, the job market, opportunities, money and a host of other things. The current world's system, as the Bible describes it, has no place for God, who is an archaic, outdated, antiquated and old-fashioned idea past its prime.

The believer, however, sees life according to a whole different worldview.

Discovering God's Assignment

Our faith informs our life choices, decisions and paths. You cannot separate your faith from who you are and what you do. Those who profess to be believers but have no life change, no evidence of faith during the week—there is no difference between them and unbelievers. There are businessmen, politicians, police officers, medical professionals and many other workers who claim to be Christians but have no idea how to live out their faith daily. They do not know their assignment from God or how to practice their faith in that assignment.

"We have been tricked into thinking there is secular, neutral ground in our lives that is neither for nor against God," writes Hugh Whelchel, senior fellow and founder of the Institute for Faith, Work & Economics. "Nothing could be further from the truth. . . . Our response to God should reverberate into every facet of life: at home, at work, in our families, in our communities, and at our churches."[2]

Look again at Abraham Kuyper's observation from the beginning of this chapter: "There is not a square inch in the whole domain of our human existence over which Christ, who is Sovereign over all, does not cry: 'Mine!'" God owns it all. And Hebrews 4:13 says: "Nothing in all creation is hidden from God's sight. Everything is uncovered and laid bare before the eyes of him to whom we must give account."

In order to understand our assignment on planet earth, we must first understand who owns it all. Revelation 4:11 says that God "created all things, and by [His] will they were created and have their being." That includes us! Our mission, purpose and assignment, then, are to reflect His glory to a lost and dying world, listening to the instructions from His Word and then following those instructions. We must do this by faith every day and all the time. Here are just a few of these instructions:

1. "Seek first the kingdom of God and his righteousness, and all these things will be added to you" (Matthew 6:33 ESV).

2. "Having put away falsehood, let each one of you speak the truth with his neighbor, for we are members one of another" (Ephesians 4:25 ESV).

3. "Be kind to one another, tenderhearted, forgiving one another, as God in Christ forgave you" (Ephesians 4:32 ESV).

4. "Do all things without grumbling or disputing, that you may be blameless and innocent, children of God without blemish in the midst of a crooked and twisted generation, among whom you shine as lights in the world" (Philippians 2:14–15 ESV).

5. "Walk in a manner worthy of the Lord, fully pleasing to him: bearing fruit in every good work and increasing in the knowledge of God" (Colossians 1:10 ESV).

6. "Keep your lives free from the love of money and be content with what you have, because God has said, 'Never will I leave you; never will I forsake you'" (Hebrews 13:5).

We do all of this by walking in trust and obeying His Word ("trust and obey," as we saw in chapter 1), following His instructions in our lives. The opposite of this is walking in unbelief—not trusting and not obeying His Word.

There is an interesting episode in the hit comedy series *Seinfeld* in which George, sitting with Jerry and Elaine in a restaurant, bemoans the following:

> It became very clear to me sitting out there today, that every decision I've ever made, in my entire life, has been wrong. My life is the opposite of everything I want it to be. Every instinct I have, in every [part] of life, be it something to wear, something to eat . . . It's all been wrong.

Then Jerry comes up with a brilliant reply: "If every instinct you have is wrong, then the opposite would have to be right."[3]

So George goes on to order chicken salad on rye, untoasted, instead of his usual tuna on toast, hoping for a change in his life's direction.

Although this scene in *Seinfeld* is funny, it is also insightful. People today are unhappy and unfulfilled because they have decided that their way is the right way. But if God's instructions to us are the right course for our lives, then not believing and not obeying His Word is wrong and even hurtful. And if Kuyper is correct that there is not a square inch in all of life that does not belong to God, then we must be about our Master's business and not our own.

Are You Afraid of God's Guidance?

Unbelief is a devastating device used by the enemy of our souls to derail us. Along with unbelief come pride, arrogance and hubris (extreme pride).

Dr. Tim Irwin published a book titled *Derailed: Five Lessons Learned from Catastrophic Failures of Leadership* that shows how high-profile CEOs of major companies got off track and were finally pushed out of their companies for isolating themselves and refusing to listen to others and follow sound advice.[4] We can be our own worst enemy.

As a family counselor, I used to ask married couples in crisis what they believed to be the foundation of their marriages. In other words, on what did they base their relationship? In most cases I received the proverbial deer-in-the-headlights look: "What are you talking about, Chaplain?" They had no clue except that they loved each other—or once did—and still wanted to be together.

If we do not base our marriages—or our very lives—on our relationship with God and His Word, we will eventually derail. If our notion of marriage is based on physical attraction or

Hollywood romance, then when those emotional highs wear off, the relationship sinks into oblivion.

And there is no true satisfaction in life without Jesus Christ. We may be tempted to think, *If only I had enough money, fame, education, the right connections, the right spouse, the right job, I would be truly happy.* But if that were true, why do some celebrities die of drug overdoses or suicide?

I have counseled people who are afraid of seeking God's guidance for their lives because they fear it will not line up with their own plans. They believe their own plans are better than God's.

Think of the pride it takes to believe that you know better than the One who designed not only you but the entire universe! No, the best course of action is to ask God if He will allow us to align with His will for our lives. Let's find out what God is doing and then join Him in it.

There was a man named Job who lost his wealth, health and most of his family. His lament was that, since he had led a righteous life, he wanted an audience with the Almighty so he could "argue [his] case with God" (Job 13:3). Well, Job got his wish. As the old saying goes, however, be careful what you wish. The argument did not go well for Job. Here was God's reply:

> "Who is this that obscures my plans with words without knowledge? Brace yourself like a man; I will question you, and you shall answer me. Where were you when I laid the earth's foundation? Tell me, if you understand. Who marked off its dimensions? Surely you know! Who stretched a measuring line across it? On what were its footings set, or who laid its cornerstone— while the morning stars sang together and all the angels shouted for joy?"
>
> Job 38:2–7

And God went on and on with His impossible questions. Job soon repented and was blessed far more than before. But our own conversations with the Almighty would sound just the same. If He designed and created us, gave us certain gifts and abilities, wired us with just the right DNA, and incorporated passion and strength into us in specific areas, then we can certainly trust Him with our future, purpose and plan.

STRATEGIC SPIRITUAL EXERCISES

1. Are there ways you separate the sacred from the secular in your own life, in areas of work, education, play, relationships and more?

2. Read God's reply to Job in Job 38–42. What do you learn from these passages? What or who is your faith in? How can you grow in your trust in God to guide your life?

3. Find Scriptures that speak to you about your faith. Start with Romans 1:17 and 10:17 and Hebrews 11.

4. Read 1 John 2:15–17. Are there areas of the world's system to which you are attached? Take these to the Lord.

5. Meditate on Kuyper's comment: "There is not a square inch in the whole domain of our human existence over which Christ, who is Sovereign over all, does not cry: 'Mine!'" Are there areas of your life you are holding back?

4

THE DNA FACTOR

There is no such thing as chance; and what seems to us merest accident springs from the deepest source of destiny.

Friedrich von Schiller, philosopher and poet, "Ode to Joy"

Early spring 1998. Fort Benning, Georgia. "Chaplain Giammona, I need you to be the chaplain for all the schools here at Fort Benning," said my boss, the installation command chaplain. "That means you'll need to go to jump school so you can fit in and be effective in your ministry to all the soldiers."

"Yes, sir," I replied, even though I had no idea what I would face by way of airborne training.

But I started at once to intensify my physical fitness training since I knew most of those in the airborne school had just come out of infantry basic training and were in top shape. I was in shape, but being older, I had to ensure that I was in top physical condition to face three weeks of intense physical wear and tear.

I reported to the first day of jump school at 0530 (5:30 a.m.) while it was still completely dark outside. There the instructors—addressed as "Sergeant Airborne" and known as "black hats" because of their black baseball caps, emblazoned with their rank and the parachutist badge, part of their training uniforms—ordered us to fall into formation. Then they commenced PT (physical training).

For the entire first week, it was continuous movement, whether in PT, jump training from 34-foot towers, the swing-landing trainer, or the numerous PLFs (parachute landing falls) that required us to drop from a zipline onto sand, hitting the ground with our boots and immediately throwing ourselves sideways to distribute the landing shock sequentially along five points of body contact with the ground.

By the end of the week, it felt as if I had hit the ground three hundred times. I was pretty banged up. I proceeded to go home for the weekend to recover, since as an officer I lived on base at Fort Benning and was not required to sleep in the barracks. I asked Esther, my wife, to pray for me. She did so, asking the Lord for His will to be done in my life.

Monday morning came around quickly—too quickly. I faced a required five-mile run, but I was sick as a dog, probably because my immune system was down. It felt like the flu. The trouble was, if you did not make the run, you were out of the program. I knew I was dehydrated and weakened by the flu. But instead of reporting to sick call, I decided to tough it out.

I don't recall where in the run it happened, but I passed out and found myself in the back of a military truck being transported to the rear.

I failed airborne training.

That episode was one of the most difficult days of my life in the Army. I felt as if my career were over. The Army can be unforgiving when it comes to failing a mission, any mission; and this failure meant not only that I could not be the chaplain for all the schools at Fort Benning, but that I would be reassigned to a non–airborne type of unit. It also meant that, in the future, I would not be assigned to some of the Army's high-speed airborne units.

I did not know it at the time, but God had other plans for me.

The brigade commander over me at the time was a great leader and did not set out to take me down. He called me to go to lunch with his staff, where he awarded me an Army achievement medal (AAM), told his troops that he liked me and my ministry, and sent me on to my next unit at Fort Benning.

Although it was not in my DNA to be airborne or special operations, God did design me for leadership. Eventually I progressed through the ranks to work at the Pentagon in Washington, D.C., achieved full colonel and became one of the senior leaders in the Army chaplaincy as the installation command chaplain supervising chaplains at more than 75 Army installations worldwide.

It is amid difficulties and failures where we learn that, if we are His followers, God rules over every event in our lives. Each of us is designed by God and given special DNA in order to fulfill our destiny—our purpose, mission and assignment.

What Is DNA?

According to the *Cambridge Dictionary*, DNA is "the chemical, present at the center of the cells of living things, that controls the structure and purpose of each cell and carries genetic information during reproduction."[1] According to Healthline, "DNA contains the instructions necessary for life," and its internal code "provides directions on how to make proteins that are vital for our growth, development, and overall health."[2]

Both of these definitions apply to our being specially created and designed by God to fulfill our assignments in life.

The military chooses people to fulfill important jobs, missions and assignments according to their talent, dispositions and gifting. The U.S. Navy Seals, the most elite special forces unit in the world, selects its ranks carefully by putting its potential personnel through the most intensive and physically demanding courses on the planet. Not everyone who applies makes it. The Seals are looking for those with the right DNA: physically strong, mentally tough and emotionally mature.

The good news is that, unlike Navy Seal applicants who are turned aside, God *did* choose each one of us! Ephesians 1:4 says, "He chose us in [Jesus Christ] before the creation of the world to be holy and blameless in his sight." And more good news: God did not choose us because of our DNA. Before we put our faith in Jesus Christ as Savior, all of us were sinners, lost sheep going our own way, living for ourselves and for our pleasures.

So why *did* God choose us? Love ("God so loved the world," John 3:16) and according to His grace alone:

> It is by grace you have been saved, through faith—and this is not from yourselves, it is the gift of God—not by works, so that no one can boast.
>
> Ephesians 2:8–9

Here is where our DNA comes in—not that we have to qualify for salvation, since not one of us measures up, but that God has placed within each one of us particular passions, skills, abilities, heart, personality and drive to fulfill the mission He pre-planned for us to accomplish. Recall this truth from chapter 1: "We are God's handiwork, created in Christ Jesus to do good works, which God prepared in advance for us to do" (Ephesians 2:10).

Just as the Navy Seals are looking for candidates with the right DNA for their elite assignment, so in the Kingdom of

God, everyone has been given the right DNA for the mission and assignment God has called him or her to—for a mission with eternal consequences.

Alex Newman, senior editor of *The New American*—a magazine that helps "[expose] media deception and political coverup," according to its website[3]—has a calling as a Christian journalist. His mission statement or motto as a Christian, he says, is found in Ephesians 5:11: "Have nothing to do with the fruitless deeds of darkness, but rather expose them." Newman explains:

> I feel beyond blessed, beyond honored, that I get to reprove and expose all day, every day, six days a week. And I will continue to do that as long as God gives me breath or until He calls me to some other assignment.
>
> We are the Body of Christ, one Body with many members, and every member has a different function. So I encourage people to be in prayer and to be reading your Bible to find out what assignment God has for you. Your assignment is probably different than mine, right? It's not for the eye to say to the ear, "Hey, what are you doing?" We've all got a job to do.[4]

Newman, also an educator and author, says all of us have different roles to play in the Great Commission, Jesus' final instruction to His disciples:

> "Go and make disciples of all nations, baptizing them in the name of the Father and of the Son and of the Holy Spirit, and teaching them to obey everything I have commanded you."
>
> Matthew 28:19–20

Newman comments:

> We need to take the Great Commission seriously, and we also need to remember the last little part—to teach others to obey all

the things Jesus has commanded us. That's important. That's discipleship. It's not just like, "Hey, here's the Gospel. All right, see you later. I'm out of here." We need to disciple people.

What does it mean to be a Christian? How do we live differently than others? What does it mean to be involved in this battle of cosmic proportions against the forces of evil, the powers and principalities described in Ephesians 6? We all have a role to play. And if you're not active in that battle, my guess is you have not yet found out where you're supposed to be. So again, be in prayer, open up your Bible and find out what God has in store for you.[5]

What Is Your DNA?

God has gifted each of us, then, with our own special DNA—gifts and talents to prepare us for our calling. We find a wonderful example of this in the Bible when God singled out Bezalel of the tribe of Judah to help make furnishings for the Tabernacle. Moses said of Bezalel:

> "[God] has filled him with the Spirit of God, with wisdom, with understanding, with knowledge and with all kinds of skills—to make artistic designs for work in gold, silver and bronze, to cut and set stones, to work in wood and to engage in all kinds of artistic crafts. And he has given both him and Oholiab son of Ahisamak, of the tribe of Dan, the ability to teach others. He has filled them with skill to do all kinds of work as engravers, designers, embroiderers in blue, purple and scarlet yarn and fine linen, and weavers—all of them skilled workers and designers."
>
> Exodus 35:31–35

Bezalel was an artist extraordinaire with the passion, drive, skill and motivation to follow God's design to make magnificent creations. What if Bezalel had decided early on that instead of becoming a skilled craftsman, he wanted to be a professional baseball player? (Work with me here!) He would have been one unhappy man since his skill set did not lie in sports but in artistry. Moreover, God had not called him to be a professional ballplayer; He called him to be an artisan and a major player in crafting God's Tabernacle in the desert.

Today many people are like that. They have not discovered who they are and what they are designed to do. It may be that circumstances of life have placed them in poverty; or they have physical deformities; or they face other types of dilemmas over which they have no control. Or they may have let fear, apathy, distrust, weakness or any number of other obstacles prevent them from accomplishing their mission. God knows our weaknesses, understands our fears, and can still help us fulfill our calling if we put our trust in Him and His Word.

Todd Smith, senior pastor of Christ Fellowship Church in Dawsonville, Georgia, talks about the origin of the North Georgia Revival and about how God helps us accomplish our mission:

> The revival started because of brokenness, because of failure. I know my position. I know who I am. I know that I can't do anything, because when Todd puts his hand on anything, it seems to lose its steam. But pastors will say, "Give me an idea. Give me a formula." So I tell them, "It's in the complete and utter destruction of who you are. It really is." But they don't want to hear that. Okay, here's the pathway. Go into a room, close the door, turn off the light and die. There are no "steps"; there's a place. Build an altar, climb up onto it, and cry out for the fire of God to consume the sacrifice.[6]

He Ran from God

Jonah, that great prophet of old, was a man gifted by God to speak prophetic words to entire kingdoms. God told him to go to Nineveh, the capital of the Assyrian Empire—the arch-enemies of Israel and one of the most ruthless, aggressive and hated nations in the history of the world. The Assyrians were known to inflict unspeakable acts of cruelty on their captives, including pulling out their tongues, skinning them alive and stacking their skulls high to instill terror in their enemies.[7] Nevertheless the Lord wanted His spokesman, Jonah, to go and preach to the Assyrians in the hope that they would repent and not go through terrible judgment.

You know that Jonah was not happy with that assignment. He knew they were cold-hearted killers, and he did not want God to forgive them; he really wanted God to annihilate them. So instead of sailing to Nineveh, he went down to Joppa and boarded a ship bound for Tarshish, in the opposite direction, "to flee from the LORD" (Jonah 1:3).

We find some interesting lessons about our purpose in the story of Jonah. First we see what happened as a result when Jonah had no intention of preaching to his enemy, the Assyrians. He knew God would have mercy on them, and his expectation of God's compassion on such a wicked enemy made him angry (see Jonah 4:2).

But things went from bad to worse when Jonah thought he could outrun God. The Bible states that he kept going down. He went "down" to Joppa, then "down" into the ship, then "down" into the hold of the ship, then he lay down to sleep, and finally—after he told the sailors that his running from God was the reason for the terrifying storm—he was thrown down into the raging sea:

> The sea was getting rougher and rougher. So they asked him, "What should we do to you to make the sea calm down for us?"
>
> "Pick me up and throw me into the sea," he replied, "and it will become calm. I know that it is my fault that this great storm has come upon you."

Instead, the men did their best to row back to land. But they could not, for the sea grew even wilder than before. Then they cried out to the LORD, "Please, LORD, do not let us die for taking this man's life. Do not hold us accountable for killing an innocent man, for you, LORD, have done as you pleased." Then they took Jonah and threw him overboard.

Jonah 1:11–15

So Jonah kept going down. That is what happens when we disobey the Lord's command and direction for our lives.

When the commander of a military unit gives a direct order, especially during war, soldiers follow those orders without question. Notice what happened when Jesus told two brothers, Simon and Andrew, to follow Him:

They were casting a net into the lake, for they were fishermen. "Come, follow me," Jesus said, "and I will send you out to fish for people." At once they left their nets and followed him.

Matthew 4:18–20

Unlike Jonah, Simon and Andrew obeyed immediately.

The second thing we notice in the Jonah story is that, when Jonah was thrown into the sea, "the raging sea grew calm. At this the men greatly feared the LORD, and they offered a sacrifice to the LORD and made vows to him" (Jonah 1:15–16).

Although the sailors had tried everything they knew to do to survive the raging storm, they failed until they asked the right question of Jonah: "What should we do to you to make the sea calm down for us?" (verse 11). We can do only so much with limited resources, thinking, abilities and education. And until we come to the place of asking God, "What should I do?" we will never find His peace, guidance, direction and blessings.

The third thing to notice in this story is that, after "the LORD provided a huge fish to swallow Jonah" (verse 17), the prophet finally came to the place of surrender and prayer:

> From inside the fish Jonah prayed to the LORD his God. He said: "In my distress I called to the LORD, and he answered me. From deep in the realm of the dead I called for help, and you listened to my cry."
>
> Jonah 2:1–2

Jonah learned to surrender inside the belly of the fish.

It is important that we come to the place of surrender in our lives as soon as possible in order to be followers of Christ.

People ask me continually, "Colonel Giammona, how were you able to face death, stress, uncertainty and fear in war?" The answer is simple: I surrendered to the Lord's instructions for my life as best as I could. I did not do it perfectly, but I gave it my all and, looking back, I have no regrets.

Our mission and purpose were appointed by God before the foundation of the world, and He has implanted the DNA in us to fulfill this mission and purpose. It is our job to listen, to trust and then to obey.

STRATEGIC SPIRITUAL EXERCISES

1. Read the entire story of Jonah (four short chapters) and ask God about your own calling in life and what He is asking you to do.

2. When you reread the Schiller quote from the beginning of this chapter—"There is no such thing as chance; and what seems to us merest accident springs from the deepest source of destiny"—can you see ways this

principle has applied and continues to apply to your path in life?

3. Read Exodus 35:30–35. What skills, abilities, passions and direction are in your DNA that God has planted within you? Write your answers down and share them with your mentor or someone you trust.

4. Ponder this whole chapter and the assignment God has gifted you with. He has given you the right DNA to accomplish this assignment. Are you willing to say yes?

5

THE WORLD'S SYSTEM

It's not about you. The purpose of your life is far greater than your own personal fulfillment, your peace of mind, or even your happiness. It's far greater than your family, your career, or even your wildest dreams and ambitions. If you want to know why you were placed on this planet, you must begin with God. You were born by his purpose and for his purpose.

Pastor Rick Warren, author, *The Purpose Driven Life*

Winter 2009. A classroom in the Pentagon, Arlington, Virginia. I could not believe what I was seeing. The chalkboards on all the walls in the classroom of more than two hundred students were filled with diagrams, schematics, charts and equations. In big, bold letters on the chalkboard in the front of the class was the title of our course for the week: "How the Army Operates!"

This was a required weeklong "force management" course on how the Army manages its force of more than one million soldiers (not including Department of the Army civilians). I turned to one of my peers sitting next to me and joked, "No wonder we can't get anything done; no one could possibly understand all this."

Evidently I was wrong, because the Department of the Army (DA) civilian trainer who conducted the class proceeded to explain every one of those diagrams and schematics over the course of the week.

The complexity was beyond comprehension. The military works in a highly organized system too complex for any one person to understand. And the force management course was just one of a multitude of courses in the Army system.

God's Kingdom—and the very universe itself—is unfathomably more complex. Hugh Ross, astrophysicist and founder of Reasons to Believe, argues that many people today scarcely realize how fine-tuned the universe is and that God is a God of immeasurable precision:

> This degree of fine tuning is so great that it's as if right after the universe's beginning someone could have destroyed the possibility of life within it by subtracting a single dime's mass from the whole observable universe or adding a single dime's mass to it.[1]

Running simultaneously on planet earth is another complex kingdom, the evil world system, operated by our enemy, the devil. During his temptation of Jesus in the wilderness, Satan said, "I will give You all this domain and its glory, for it has been handed over to me, and I give it to whomever I want" (Luke 4:6 NASB). It is true, the world *was* handed over to Satan when Adam and Eve fell. His kingdom, including the evil world system, is all around us, yet most of us little know or perceive it.

It is much like the movie *The Matrix*, in which computer hacker Neo is led to a dark underworld and finds the awful truth—that the life he knows is the intricate deception of an "evil cyber-intelligence" system. Neo joins legendary and dangerous rebel warrior Morpheus in the battle to destroy the illusion enslaving humanity.[2]

We were "rescued . . . from the domain of darkness, and transferred . . . to the kingdom of His beloved Son, in whom we have redemption, the forgiveness of sins" (Colossians 1:13–14 NASB) when we received Jesus Christ as Savior. But there are many unbelievers—and some believers as well—who place their trust and their future in the world's system composed of people under the influence of Satan and his rule of the earth.

Beware of Fitting In

I was in my first college class at California State University, Sacramento, the introduction to anthropology. The first thing out of the professor's mouth was that Adam and Eve were a myth, the Bible was not accurate, and science, not religion, has all the answers for mankind.

Many in the class, I am sure, found that acceptable, but I was not having any of it. I argued with that professor the entire semester and, if I remember correctly, was fortunate to receive a C.

By the grace of God, I did not lose my faith in college (although I was a brand-new Christian as of about nine months). But many church kids who attend secular educational institutions do, and come out agnostics or atheists. Liberal colleges and universities are part and parcel of the dark world system on our planet today.

It is important for us to understand, then, that as followers of Christ, we must not be pulled into the way the world understands its assignments and mission; we must continue to allow Jesus to work in our lives to accomplish His will. The world, which is at enmity with God, tells us to accumulate wealth, power, prestige and fame so we can become powerful people.

What the world does *not* tell us is what will happen if we do not repent and follow Christ. Jesus said:

> "Whoever wants to be my disciple must deny themselves and take up their cross and follow me. For whoever wants to save their life will lose it, but whoever loses their life for me and for the gospel will save it. What good is it for someone to gain the whole world, yet forfeit their soul?"
>
> Mark 8:34–36

If you are enslaved by the world's system, you will lose your soul for all eternity, because the world and its system are at odds with God and His Kingdom. We were not meant to be popular in the eyes of our culture. Jesus said, "You do not belong to the world, but I have chosen you out of the world. That is why the world hates you" (John 15:19).

Denying ourselves means not following our own desires but following the One who has destined us to live with Him forever. God has purposed us to live differently from the world. That means we need to stop trying to fit into the culture, trying to please those who are destined for eternal destruction.

This kind of fitting in and accommodating has happened throughout the history of Israel and the Church. Israel, when led by godly leaders, followed the Lord, but afterward she fell into the sins of the pagan nations around her. It happened repeatedly. It is why Assyria was able to carry the Israelites into exile in the eighth century BC:

> All this took place because the Israelites had sinned against the LORD their God, who had brought them up out of Egypt from under the power of Pharaoh king of Egypt. They worshiped other gods and followed the practices of the nations the LORD had driven out before them, as well as the practices that the kings of Israel had introduced.

The Israelites secretly did things against the LORD their God that were not right. From watchtower to fortified city they built themselves high places in all their towns. They set up sacred stones and Asherah poles on every high hill and under every spreading tree. At every high place they burned incense, as the nations whom the LORD had driven out before them had done. They did wicked things that aroused the LORD's anger. They worshiped idols, though the LORD had said, "You shall not do this."

2 Kings 17:7–12

What happened to Israel, and later Judah? The people became like the nations around them. They intermarried with those living in the countries surrounding them, although the Lord had warned them not to do this, and they ended up serving idols instead of the one true God. They did not understand that they had become like the idols they were worshiping—blind, deaf and dumb (see Psalm 115:4–8).

Jesus' Warning

What about today? Look at the decline of many of the mainstream churches and denominations. Most of these church organizations, which started out with power, revival, discipline and stamina, are little more than distortions of their former selves. Why? Here is the cycle: They start with power and enthusiasm while being ostracized by the world. They grow by spreading God's Word and making disciples. They become more educated and even sophisticated by building denominational headquarters and schools. The rest of the Church and the world accept their "improvements." Then starts their decline into the culture, until they become part of the world's system.

Jesus warned five of the seven churches in the book of Revelation that convenience, complacency or compromise would lead to their demise. Look at what Jesus says in His message to the church at Ephesus in Revelation 2:4–5:

> "I hold this against you: You have forsaken the love you had at first. Consider how far you have fallen! Repent and do the things you did at first. If you do not repent, I will come to you and remove your lampstand from its place."

Eric Metaxas, a *New York Times* bestselling author and host of the nationally syndicated *Eric Metaxas Radio Show*, sees a striking parallel between the American Church today and the Church in Germany before World War II:

> That's no exaggeration, not even slightly. The reason it's important for me to say that is because a lot of people are disinclined to believe that the American Church is exactly where the German Church was as the Nazis took power. That's because most Americans, when they think of the Nazis, don't think of what it was like at that early stage, say in 1933, but of where it all went and what happened and the nightmare of the Holocaust.
>
> We need to forget about that and take ourselves back to the time before the Holocaust, when many Germans had no idea and could never dream where it was headed. Maybe they didn't like the Nazis, but they didn't think the Nazis taking over was worth making any trouble about. They thought, *We'll just play nice, and the pendulum swings back and forth, and we'll be fine.*
>
> Well, that's obviously not how it went. There were very few people—German Lutheran pastor and anti-Nazi dissident Dietrich Bonhoeffer was one of those few—who saw where things could go and actually would go if the Church did not speak up and fight back and refuse to bow the knee to the secular Nazi state.[3]

Many reasons were given, says Metaxas, for the Church in Germany to go along and not fight back, including the widespread belief that Romans 13 requires blind submission to the government:

> Let everyone be subject to the governing authorities, for there is no authority except that which God has established. The authorities that exist have been established by God.
>
> Romans 13:1

But Metaxas says emphatically:

> They got it wrong. Anybody who's read my *Bonhoeffer* book knows the nightmare that was unleashed because they got it wrong—because of the silence of the Church. How could the Church get it so wrong and fail to see what happened? The answer is they got it wrong and were silent—as I say in my book *Letter to the American Church*—exactly as we Americans are getting it wrong right now. It started exactly the same way.
>
> It's not even like we're in the beginning, really. We're more in the middle of it right now. So I want the Church to wake up and hear the warning, because there's nothing more horrible than the Lord calling His Church to be His Church and they say, "Not yet. Not yet. We're not ready. We're really doing just fine. We don't want to get radical." That is where the German Church was, and we saw what happened. And that is precisely where the American Church is today.[4]

Complacency and "going along" happens not only to churches and denominations but to individuals as well. Many young people raised in God-fearing homes and churches who venture out into the world's system for which they are not prepared—including higher education, as I have said—eventually find themselves in rebellion against their families and even against God.

My main point in this chapter is this: If you mean to follow Jesus Christ in the mission, assignment and purpose He has for you, you must not get pulled into the world's system. It will offer many tempting opportunities that look good for you. But remember Jesus' warning to those first-century churches.

Long-time motivational speaker Jim Rohn once said, "If you don't design your own life plan, chances are you'll fall into someone else's plan. And guess what they have planned for you? Not much."[5]

What Jim meant by that, if you were to ask him, is that the divine plan is the only plan. If you slip away from God's plan for your life in favor of the world's system and its tempting offerings, you will regret it.

Standing Against the World System

A great example of not being pulled into the world's system is found in the life and story of Nehemiah, Jewish cupbearer to King Artaxerxes around 445 BC.

A cupbearer not only serves wine to the king, but tastes it first to make sure it is not poisoned. This was a "secular" job in the eyes of the world, but not so for Nehemiah. It was his sacred duty to serve the Persian king, and God had placed him there—in a high position in the king's court, favored by King Artaxerxes—for a particular calling.

The Power of Prayer

When Nehemiah found out that the walls of Jerusalem, back home in Judah, were broken down and the gates burned with fire, he wept and fasted for "some days" (Nehemiah 1:4). Then he prayed:

"Lord, the God of heaven, the great and awesome God, who keeps his covenant of love with those who love him and keep his commandments, let your ear be attentive and your eyes open to hear the prayer your servant is praying before you day and night for your servants, the people of Israel. I confess the sins we Israelites, including myself and my father's family, have committed against you. We have acted very wickedly toward you. We have not obeyed the commands, decrees and laws you gave your servant Moses."

verses 5–7

And righteous Nehemiah went on to confess and intercede for his fellow Israelites.

Prayer is the key to our assignment from God. The assignment is not automatic, meaning we do nothing and God does everything. No, we are in partnership with the Almighty. And many times we find that God places the answers to our prayers within us, once we decide to put feet to our faith.

This is what happened with Nehemiah.

Following Up Prayer

We find the answer to Nehemiah's prayers in the next chapter, when the king asked him why his face looked sad:

I was very much afraid, but I said to the king, "May the king live forever! Why should my face not look sad when the city where my ancestors are buried lies in ruins, and its gates have been destroyed by fire?"

The king said to me, "What is it you want?"

Then I prayed to the God of heaven, and I answered the king, "If it pleases the king and if your servant has found favor in his sight, let him send me to the city in Judah where my ancestors are buried so that I can rebuild it."

> Then the king, with the queen sitting beside him, asked me, "How long will your journey take, and when will you get back?" It pleased the king to send me; so I set a time.
>
> Nehemiah 2:2–6

It does no good to pray and then not do what God directs us to do. In the case of Nehemiah, we find that he prayed, then was given an open door to the king—but it was not cut and dried. Notice that he "was very much afraid" since he looked sad in front of the king. It is well known that you were always to be at your best and never sad or upset in the presence of a monarch; it could cost you your life if he was in a bad mood himself.

Even when you pray and then follow through, you may find yourself in dire circumstances, much as Nehemiah grieved over the condition of Jerusalem. He acted on his faith in God, however, and told the king boldly why he was sad, even though he did this in fear and trepidation. He never took counsel from his fear but relied on his faith and continued to pray, even as he made his request to the king. It worked!

Although Nehemiah lived and worked in the court of the Persian king, he did not belong to that world's system. He was not caught up in the pomp and intrigue of the high court; he remained faithful to the one true God, in spite of having advanced to the top of his profession, with money and prestige. Nehemiah knew his mission, assignment and focus.

Asking the king for permission to go was just the beginning of his mission. He had a long way to go.

> I also said to him, "If it pleases the king, may I have letters to the governors of Trans-Euphrates, so that they will provide me safe-conduct until I arrive in Judah? And may I have a letter to Asaph, keeper of the royal park, so he will give me timber to

make beams for the gates of the citadel by the temple and for the city wall and for the residence I will occupy?"

Nehemiah 2:7–8

Nehemiah understood that he needed more than the king's permission to leave and do what was in his heart, to rebuild the walls around Jerusalem. He also needed safe passage and resources. He knew that, when you are in the presence of the king, ask for everything you need because you just might get it! There is an old saying based on the Bible: "Where God guides, He provides." Nehemiah wrote, "And because the gracious hand of my God was on me, the king granted my requests" (verse 8).

Handling Opposition

As with all missions and assignments in life, Nehemiah ran into roadblocks. Sometimes God allows these to see where we are placing our faith.

Nehemiah arrived in Jerusalem, surveyed the damage and brought the Jewish officials up to speed. They responded, "Let us start rebuilding" (verse 18). Then came the roadblocks:

> But when Sanballat the Horonite, Tobiah the Ammonite official and Geshem the Arab heard about it, they mocked and ridiculed us. "What is this you are doing?" they asked. "Are you rebelling against the king?"
>
> I answered them by saying, "The God of heaven will give us success. We his servants will start rebuilding, but as for you, you have no share in Jerusalem or any claim or historic right to it."

Nehemiah 2:19–20

The opposition grew stronger and more dangerous, until Nehemiah "posted a guard day and night" (Nehemiah 4:9) and prepared to meet the threat:

> Half of my men did the work, while the other half were equipped with spears, shields, bows and armor. . . . Those who carried materials did their work with one hand and held a weapon in the other, and each of the builders wore his sword at his side as he worked.
>
> Nehemiah 4:16–18

Nehemiah's mission to rebuild the walls around Jerusalem involved moving the obstacles in front of them—persuading the people not only to build but to overcome the enemy.

Notice that Nehemiah did not try to make friends with those enemies. He made the following response four times to their threats: "I am carrying on a great project and cannot go down. Why should the work stop while I leave it and go down to you?" (Nehemiah 6:3). In other words, Nehemiah simply told them to bug off because he had work to do!

In just 52 days, Nehemiah and the people finished rebuilding the wall. It was quite an accomplishment for a cupbearer to the Persian king. He accomplished the mission God put into his heart because of his refusal to compromise with the world, and because of his faith, focus and perseverance.

Resisting the World's System

Sometimes it seems that a mission or assignment will never come to fruition, but the key is to never give up. If you are experiencing difficulties, obstacles or problems, do the next thing, little by little, and if God is directing you, you will progress and succeed.

What about opposition? Many churches today make a mistake by asking unbelievers what they want in a service so they can be comfortable. Many individuals make a mistake by trying to appease everyone around them instead of pleasing God. That is the wrong approach, not true to the Gospel.

But if you understand and resist the world's system, you will succeed in fulfilling God's overall plan, purpose and assignments in your life.

═══ STRATEGIC SPIRITUAL EXERCISES ═══

1. What worldly ideas and principles do you need to discard today?
2. Read Jesus' messages to the seven churches in Revelation 2–3. Are there actions, attitudes or ideas you need to repent of?
3. Read through the book of Nehemiah and write down insights on this leader's character traits, strategies and how he handled opposition. Are there principles you can implement in your own life?
4. What task or assignment has God given you to accomplish that you have not started yet? Why not start now?

PART 2

THE FAITH WALK

6

LIVING OUT FAITH
IN THE REAL WORLD

These are the men who took the cliffs. These are the champions who helped free a continent. These are the heroes who helped end a war.

President Ronald Reagan, Pointe du Hoc, France, June 6, 1984, commemorating the Normandy invasion

Winter 1993. A road to Hohenfels, Germany, on the way to the Combat Maneuver Training Center (CMTC). When things can go wrong, they often do. That is my version of Murphy's Law, and this morning is no different.

My chaplain assistant is driving—actually, speeding—our Humvee toward my first staff meeting in the field with my new commander before our entry into the realistic training area called "the box" for intense training at CMTC. I am new to the unit, I want to ensure a good first impression, and this is an important training event. I do not want to be late.

Then I notice smoke coming out from under the hood of our vehicle, but I say, "Don't stop, Sergeant, whatever you do! I can't be late for this meeting!"

So instead of slowing down, my sergeant presses the pedal to the metal and speeds up, as smoke billows out of the engine. It looks like an old black-and-white slapstick comedy film starring Laurel and Hardy. Then we come barreling into the motor pool where, of all people, the grizzled motor sergeant is standing, hands on hips, gaping at us, his jaw dropping. He proceeds to let out a string of expletives consisting of words not found in the Bible.

"What in the [blankety blank] are you doing to my Humvee? Do you know how many weeks it's going to take for me to fix this [blankety blank] vehicle?"

I bound away for the meeting, which I make just in the nick of time, leaving my sergeant to deal with the mess.

Things go wrong all the time, just as I experienced that day. We could have stopped and spent hours trying to get the vehicle towed and fixed. But my mission of the day was to get to that important planning session with the new commander (although I did feel bad for the poor motor sergeant who would have to slave away on that vehicle for several weeks).

Sometimes in the real world we must make hard choices. We must sacrifice to accomplish the task at hand. It is not always cut and dried or easy.

There are always unknowns—obstacles, opposition and unforeseen circumstances—that cloud our vision and block our path. It may be a lack of funds, a difficult relationship or any number of distresses, as Jesus said: "In the world you will have tribulation; but be of good cheer, I have overcome the world" (John 16:33 NKJV).

The military plans according to the mission at hand, whether it is an amphibious assault, an airborne invasion, a night infiltration or any number of tactical operations. It plans the number of troops, vehicles, rations, munitions, weapons and more. But there will be unknown, unplanned elements in every given operation—how the enemy reacts and any number of unforeseeable circumstances. This is the real world where things go bad.

The Most Dangerous Mission

Although the concept of Murphy's Law has been around for centuries, Edward Aloysius Murphy Jr., an American aerospace engineer who worked on safety-critical systems, is often cited as the originator: "Anything that can go wrong will go wrong."

The military is known for espousing Murphy's Law. One of the most horrific examples of things going wrong took place on D-Day, June 6, 1944, during the successful Allied invasion of western Europe against Adolf Hitler in World War II.

The 2nd Ranger Battalion, at the time one of the U.S. Army's most elite units, had planned and trained rigorously for the assault on Pointe du Hoc above the beaches of Normandy during this largest seaborne invasion in history. After landing they would have to scale hundred-foot cliffs with grappling hooks, ropes and ladders to destroy a battery of 155-millimeter artillery guns pointed at the beaches below, where the Allied invasion was to take place. The Rangers would have to overcome the German forces defending the cliffs with small arms fire, mortars and grenades.[1]

"Anything that can go wrong will go wrong" became an understatement for this mission. In war as in life, timing is everything.

Several mishaps happened at the same time. Three companies (seventy men per company) of Lieutenant Colonel James Earl Rudder's 2nd Ranger Battalion were to land at Pointe du Hoc at 6:30 a.m. on June 6, but were delayed by rough sea conditions. Then two landing craft were lost, one of them disabled by enemy fire. But the Rangers debarked and started up the cliffs, supported by the Allied destroyer *USS Satterlee*.[2]

And more went wrong:

> Inching their way toward the rocky summit, the Rangers dodged rifle fire, grenades, and rocks from the German defenders above. After suffering appalling casualties, the Rangers finally made it to the top of the ominous cliff. Moments later, elation turned to disbelief as the GIs discovered that the big gun emplacements atop Pointe du Hoc were empty.[3]

After all the work, trouble, planning, stress and casualties, those 155-millimeter artillery pieces they had scaled the cliff to take out were not there. They had been moved and hidden by the Germans. But after two days of fighting, relieved by Lieutenant Colonel Max F. Schneider's 5th Ranger Battalion, the 2nd Rangers found and destroyed the guns.

Only about ninety out of more than two hundred men survived.[4]

General Omar Bradley, then commander of the U.S. 12th Army Group, observed, "It was the most dangerous mission of D-Day."[5] But the mission was accomplished, and the Rangers took pride in their achievement despite the overwhelming odds and unexpected failures along the way.

As believers in a good God—a God of love, compassion and forbearance toward His children—how do we navigate all the bad things that happen as we pursue Him and His plan for our lives? How do we live out our faith in the real world?

The Problem of Evil

We know that bad things happen. Soldiers are wounded or killed in battle, loved ones get sick, children die, plans go awry, any number of events go sour. This is where faith meets the real world.

The Bible does not sugarcoat or whitewash the accounts of the heroes of our faith. Bad things happen. But people of faith look beyond their present circumstances and into the eternal Kingdom:

> And what more shall I say? I do not have time to tell about Gideon, Barak, Samson and Jephthah, about David and Samuel and the prophets, who through faith conquered kingdoms, administered justice, and gained what was promised; who shut the mouths of lions, quenched the fury of the flames, and escaped the edge of the sword; whose weakness was turned to strength; and who became powerful in battle and routed foreign armies. Women received back their dead, raised to life again. There were others who were tortured, refusing to be released so that they might gain an even better resurrection. Some faced jeers and flogging, and even chains and imprisonment. They were put to death by stoning; they were sawed in two; they were killed by the sword. They went about in sheepskins and goatskins, destitute, persecuted and mistreated—the world was not worthy of them. They wandered in deserts and mountains, living in caves and in holes in the ground.
>
> Hebrews 11:32–38

Like these heroes of faith—although "none of them received what had been promised" (verse 39)—we, too, must press on in the face of unexpected obstacles and adverse circumstances. It is in the difficult times, the times when our faith is tested, that we grow to trust God. Pressing on is not only a key military way of getting things done, but it is at the heart of accomplishing our mission in God's army, and it has a strong biblical foundation.

Here is how Jesus faced the unimaginable mission of going to the cross:

Jesus went out as usual to the Mount of Olives, and his disciples followed him. On reaching the place, he said to them, "Pray that you will not fall into temptation." He withdrew about a stone's throw beyond them, knelt down and prayed, "Father, if you are willing, take this cup from me; yet not my will, but yours be done." An angel from heaven appeared to him and strengthened him. And being in anguish, he prayed more earnestly, and his sweat was like drops of blood falling to the ground.

Luke 22:39–44

From the beginning of time, Jesus knew He must go to the cross and die for the sins of mankind. That was His mission. Yet at this crucial crossroads, He prayed to the Father that "this cup," meaning the journey to crucifixion for the sins of all mankind, might be taken from Him. Every man and woman, boy and girl who has ever lived needs Jesus to have bled and died on the cross on their behalf, so they can enter heaven. No cross, no salvation. But Jesus pressed on and the rest is history. Thank God!

There are countless stories of evangelists, laypersons and martyrs who have pressed on amid trying circumstances. Paul, that great apostle of old, had this to say about pressing on:

Brothers and sisters, I do not consider myself yet to have taken hold of it. But one thing I do: Forgetting what is behind and straining toward what is ahead, I press on toward the goal to win the prize for which God has called me heavenward in Christ Jesus.

Philippians 3:13–14

Here is a man who was shipwrecked, beaten with rods, falsely accused, thrown into prison, whipped, stoned, stranded in the sea, and who endured many other sufferings. His eyes were on the prize.

Another great missionary, William Carey, never gave up although he saw no conversions in India for seven years. Carey's young son Peter died of dysentery, and his wife's mental health deteriorated until she died in 1807. "This is indeed the valley of the shadow of death to me," Carey wrote at the time. "But I rejoice that I am here notwithstanding; and God is here."[6] Carey remained in India, translated the Bible into Bengali and several other dialects, joined his missionary associates in baptizing many converts, and inspired countless believers in generations to follow to answer God's call to missions.[7] William Carey has been called the father of modern missions.

Alex Newman, the award-winning journalist, educator and author, points out that there are many ways for believers to deal with roadblocks and obstacles in order to fulfill our divine assignments:

Prayer is incredibly significant. I don't think we can be involved in a spiritual war without constantly being in prayer. The Bible tells us to be in prayer about everything. In good times and in bad, we should be asking God for everything.

But ultimately we need to focus on the end. There are going to be sufferings; there will be persecution. My goodness, go read *Foxe's Book of Martyrs*. Our brothers and sisters for two thousand years have been fed to lions and tortured brutally. But we need to "count it all joy" that we could be so honored as to suffer for our Lord, our Savior and our King, Jesus Christ.

So anytime you're going through a tough time, anytime something seems insurmountable, just recognize that these struggles and challenges actually build character. They help us persevere. They help build our faith. And ultimately we can be grateful because they help us become more effective servants and adopted children of the Most High.[8]

It is hard to feel grateful for the trials and tribulations of life. But Newman adds:

> It almost sounds cliché, but remember that all things work for the good of those who love the Lord and have been called according to His purpose. I've seen that in my own life. Some of the things that have seemed the most catastrophic, I look back on now and see that, oh my goodness, God used them in such an amazing way. I wouldn't want it any other way.
>
> You may not see it at the time, but have faith that God's Word is true. God is faithful, and what He has promised, you can take to the bank.[9]

Completing the Mission

Many see the life of Samson, legendary Israelite warrior and judge renowned for his prodigious strength, as a failure, an example of what not to do. But there is a redeeming side to his life as well. Yes, Samson had serious sinful habits and attitudes, including anger, not something we want to emulate. But his story is in the Bible for a reason, and he is named as one of those heroes in Hebrews 11 "who through faith conquered kingdoms" (verse 33).

God's redeeming grace, even at the end of a life not lived for His glory, is stronger than our rebellion and sin if we will just turn to Him, even in our last moments of life. Samson is a great example.

Let's look at the beginning of Samson's life:

> A certain man of Zorah, named Manoah, from the clan of the Danites, had a wife who was childless, unable to give birth. The angel of the LORD appeared to her and said, "You are barren and childless, but you are going to become pregnant and give birth to a son. Now see to it that you drink no wine or other

fermented drink and that you do not eat anything unclean. You will become pregnant and have a son whose head is never to be touched by a razor because the boy is to be a Nazirite, dedicated to God from the womb. He will take the lead in delivering Israel from the hands of the Philistines."

Judges 13:2–5

Right off the bat we see that Samson was called by God supernaturally, through the angel of the Lord, and that his mission was to lead Israel out of bondage. God would give Samson supernatural strength to defeat the Philistines.

I love that the Bible pulls no punches. It lays it out for all to see—the good, the bad and the ugly. Samson made many sinful choices in the years to come. He insisted on marrying a Philistine woman against the wishes of his parents (although Judges 14:4 tells us that "this was from the LORD, who was seeking an occasion to confront the Philistines"). Samson killed thirty men just to get their clothes to give to those he made a bet with. He slept with a prostitute. And he did many other sordid things. Yet God had called Samson to lead Israel and deliver her.

When Samson was fooled into giving up the secret of his strength—his uncut hair—through the wiles of Delilah, he was led into captivity, blinded and made a slave by the Philistines. Yet Samson did not give up. "The hair on his head began to grow again after it had been shaved" (Judges 16:22). And when he was brought out to perform for the jeering Philistine leaders in the temple of their god, Dagon, God gave strength to the now-blinded judge of Israel one more time to take down the Philistines:

When they stood him among the pillars, Samson said to the servant who held his hand, "Put me where I can feel the pillars that support the temple, so that I may lean against them." Now the temple was crowded with men and women; all the rulers of the Philistines were there, and on the roof were about three thousand men and women watching Samson perform.

Then Samson prayed to the LORD, "Sovereign LORD, remember me. Please, God, strengthen me just once more, and let me with one blow get revenge on the Philistines for my two eyes." Then Samson reached toward the two central pillars on which the temple stood. Bracing himself against them, his right hand on the one and his left hand on the other, Samson said, "Let me die with the Philistines!" Then he pushed with all his might, and down came the temple on the rulers and all the people in it. Thus he killed many more when he died than while he lived.

Judges 16:25–30

God, in His wisdom, mercy and providence, gave Samson supernatural strength one more time at the end of his life. So Samson finished well and accomplished the mission God had given him, through the angel, before the beginning of his life.

It is important that we finish well. Samson made many mistakes and committed many sins, but God was still able to use him to deliver Israel from the Philistines.

Life has many twists and turns, ups and downs. Life is messy, unpredictable and often uncontrollable. You may think you have control over your life until the first major disease, economic upheaval or other calamity hits, when you realize that your control over your life is an illusion.

It is important that, even when things go wrong, you continue to trust and obey God. Like the soldiers in the 2nd Ranger Battalion, press on with the mission and trust God for the results. Results do not always look like victory on this side of heaven. We cannot see as God sees. He sees the beginning from the end. So we must trust Him even when things do not look good.

We have all heard stories of missionaries going to faraway places to preach the Gospel with few to no results, and then dying. Years later, however, the results come to the forefront.

Nate Saint and Jim Elliot were two of five missionaries to the Auca Indians in Ecuador (who called themselves the Huaorani), in eager pursuit of bringing the Gospel to this inhospitable and murderous people. The Huaoranis speared the five missionaries to death in 1956 before they got to engage them with the truths of the Bible. But two years later, in 1958, Nate's sister, Rachel, and Jim's widow, Elisabeth, took up the mantle of the mission to the Huaorani tribe, and many of the Indians came to faith in Jesus Christ.[10]

God always has a plan. We can trust Him.

Resisting Tyranny

Today the Body of Christ needs more people like Nate Saint and Jim Elliot, brave warriors of God willing to trust God completely and put the Lord's call on their lives ahead of themselves.

Eric Metaxas says there is a "one hundred percent chance that we will lose our freedoms, and things will get unspeakably worse than they are now if the Church does not speak up and act up and push back hard" against powerful forces seeking to silence her and usher in woke tyranny. Metaxas explains:

> Understand that there is no doubt that we are on that path right now. Again, some people might think I'm exaggerating, that I'm speaking hyperbolically, dramatically. But there is no question that we have atrophied to the point where we don't have those muscles, and we need to get them back quickly. There are churches and Christian leaders who have been heroic, but most have not. Most have said, "We're going to take a pass. We don't want to be political. We don't want to be divisive." They are not understanding the times.

But if you want to pretend it's still 1985 or 1995 or even 2005—as though everything is fine—you're a fool and God will hold you responsible. Many, many of the Germans before World War II who refused to see the evil that had come upon them lived to regret it. And it was a very, very, very bitter regret. But that is exactly where we are now.

People often say, "How did it happen in Germany? How is it possible that a Christian nation, a culturally sophisticated nation, could have allowed that to happen?" And I reply, It happened exactly as it is happening right now before our eyes. People are looking the other way. "I don't want to lose my job. I don't want to lose a friendship. I don't want to get canceled. I don't want to get in trouble. I don't want to have my 501(c)(3) status threatened. I don't want somebody to walk out of my church because I'm being too political." They're not being led by biblical faith in the God of the Scripture. They're being led by fear. And you say, "How did it happen then?" It happened then exactly as it's happening now. Some of the details are different, but basically it's the same thing.[11]

The Bible is explicit that in the end times, things will get difficult. Tough choices lie ahead for those who follow Christ. Jesus gives us hope, however, when He says, "Be of good cheer; I have overcome the world" (John 16:33 KJV).

STRATEGIC SPIRITUAL EXERCISES

1. As you consider the calling and life of Samson, what do you sense God saying to you?
2. Look at some of the past problems and obstacles in your life. What did you think about them at the time? Now, as you look back, what has changed?

3. Read Luke 22:39–44 and the travail of Jesus in the Garden of Gethsemane. Why did Jesus ask the Father to take the cup from Him? How might you apply His prayer to some difficulty you are facing today?

4. Consider a few of your past accomplishments. How did they make you feel at the time? Are there ways those accomplishments might help you with your current assignment?

7

DEVELOPING YOUR FAITH

Faith comes by hearing, and hearing by the word of God.

Romans 10:17 NKJV

Summer 2006. Presidential Tower, 12th floor, Crystal City, Virginia. "Welcome, Chaplain Giammona, to your new assignment as the IMCOM's personnel manager," says my new boss.

"Thanks, sir," I reply.

"There are your seat and computer station over there, so go ahead and get to work."

That is pretty much how I entered the world of assignment management for the U.S. Army Chaplain Corps. I had just come out of Kuwait for a year and been selected for promotion to lieutenant colonel and reassigned to the Pentagon as the chaplain personnel manager for IMCOM, U.S. Army Installation Management Command. Later I would be transferred as the personnel assignments officer for the chief of chaplains.

The truth is, I had no idea what I was doing or how to do it. I attended one personnel assignments conference for a week in

Texas. That was it. My new boss was content just to watch me and see if I had what it took to do my job.

My motto in those days, and still is today: *Fake it till you make it.* For me that meant going through the motions, acting as if I knew what I was doing, and asking lots of questions, to see if somehow, with the help of the Lord, things might possibly work out.

It was a stressful time in many ways. I had just moved into a new house and settled my family into a new routine and new schools. I was delving into a new job and a new community and a new church all at the same time. But these stresses developed my faith because there was no way I would make it without God.

People ask all the time how to develop their faith. There is no simple answer, but there is one thing I know: Faith grows in the crucible of stress and hard times, which includes obstacles, roadblocks and uphill battles. (We discussed some of those in the last chapter.)

There is no way a new first lieutenant chaplain can do the job of a full colonel. Why? Because he lacks the experience, knowledge, testing, relationships and everything else needed to function at that level. It is so with developing faith as well. It grows by hearing and obeying the Word of God daily—a gradual process of allowing God to work in your life.

In the Army, if you lack confidence and conviction in your training, leadership and equipment, you will probably not survive in combat. In the same way, developing faith under pressure comes through the daily routine of trusting in God, His Word and His purpose for you.

Listening to God

In his book *Created to Dream*, Pastor Rick Warren, founder of Saddleback Church in Lake Forest, California, describes the process God uses to grow our faith, develop our character and turn our God-given dreams into reality. This faith-building process, Warren writes,

> will be repeated over and over in your life as God keeps moving you toward spiritual and emotional maturity. The growth process begins with dreaming, but dreaming is just the first phase. There are five more phases, and if you don't understand the many ways that dreams (and your faith) will be tested, you'll be tempted to give up. But dreaming is the step that gets the ball rolling. It is a catalyst for personal change. And that is what God is more concerned about: preparing you for life with him in eternity.
>
> Here's a little secret: while you are more interested in reaching your dream on earth, God is more interested in building your character for heaven. Why? Because God has long-range plans for you that will far outlast your brief time on earth. God has a longer view of you. He's looking at your life in light of eternity. The fact is this: any goal or dream that you envision happening here on earth will be short-term because everything on earth is temporary. We're just passing through. This is just the warm-up act before the real show takes place on the other side of death. Life on earth doesn't last. But life in eternity will last forever.[1]

Part of building our character is growing in faith, which is required for our mission and assignments in life. When we walk daily with the Lord, we develop our ability to hear His voice, and in time we are tuned in to that voice.

This short story from Genesis is a powerful example of walking with God by faith:

> When Enoch had lived 65 years, he became the father of Methuselah. After he became the father of Methuselah, Enoch walked faithfully with God 300 years and had other sons and

daughters. Altogether, Enoch lived a total of 365 years. *Enoch walked faithfully with God; then he was no more, because God took him away.*

Genesis 5:21–24, emphasis added

We know little about the life of Enoch, but we do know that he walked faithfully with God for three hundred years. In fact, his life of faith pleased God so much that God translated him to heaven apart from death.

We see this restated in Hebrews 11:5 (NASB):

By faith Enoch was taken up so that he would not see death; and he was not found because God took him up; for before he was taken up, he was attested to have been pleasing to God.

There is some speculation that Enoch may be one of the two witnesses, along with Elijah, who will come back to earth just before Christ's return, since they are the only two Bible heroes who did not see death, but were taken up directly to heaven:

I will appoint my two witnesses, and they will prophesy for 1,260 days, clothed in sackcloth. They are "the two olive trees" and the two lampstands, and "they stand before the Lord of the earth." If anyone tries to harm them, fire comes from their mouths and devours their enemies. This is how anyone who wants to harm them must die. They have power to shut up the heavens so that it will not rain during the time they are prophesying; and they have power to turn the waters into blood and to strike the earth with every kind of plague as often as they want.

Revelation 11:3–6

These two witnesses will be killed "when they have finished their testimony" (verse 7), and their deaths will be celebrated by many—but they will return to life after three and a half days and be called "up to heaven in a cloud" (verse 12), while their enemies look on.

Whether or not one of these two witnesses will be Enoch, we know that he walked so closely to God by faith that he was given a new assignment in heaven. We can imagine that during those three hundred years of walking with God, Enoch's faith was tried and tested. But we know from Scripture that he never gave up; he continued his journey until his mission on earth was accomplished.

It is important that we, too, as the people of God, strive to walk with Him by faith every moment of every day. If we do, we know He will be pleased with us—and who knows what journey He will take us on, and what joy we will experience, as we place our full confidence in the One who made us?

"Consider God as the big personnel manager in your life," says retired U.S. Army Chaplain (Colonel) Scott McChrystal. "He's the One who sent you where you are. He's the One who monitors your career. He knows what's best. And He doesn't mind throwing in an occasional surprise! Most of my assignments in the military were surprises."[2]

How do we handle the surprises that come our way? With faith.

Eric Metaxas says certain key Scriptures have helped him in his faith journey, especially those emphasizing the importance of prayer. He says:

> One of the Scriptures is Philippians 4:6: "Be anxious for nothing, but in everything by prayer and supplication, with thanksgiving, let your requests be made known to God" (NKJV). Why does the Word of God command us to be anxious for nothing? Because the normal thing is to be anxious.
>
> There are all kinds of reasons to worry and be fearful. And the Lord says, "I get it. I understand. But the moment you have that temptation, My Word says, 'Be anxious for nothing.' So give it to me in prayer. Take every problem and bring it to the

foot of My cross. Give it to Me, your heavenly Father." It's the only way to live. Otherwise we internalize these things and worry and torture ourselves. I do that, too—but it's sin, and the Lord wants us to be free.

And Romans 8:28: "All things work together for good to those who love God, to those who are the called according to His purpose." Even when a bad thing happens, say, "Lord, I praise You. I know that You alone have the ability to take this bad thing and do something beautiful with it."

We need to live with that kind of faith every day. If we don't, not only are we going to suffer, but God's purposes in our lives are going to suffer.

These Scriptures help me almost on a daily basis.[3]

Stepping Out of the Boat

As we listen to God through His Word, we learn much about the life of faith from Peter.

Simon Peter was hand-picked by Jesus, along with James and John. They would be His three closest disciples. But Peter stands out from among them. On Mount Tabor, the Mount of Transfiguration, Jesus brought these three with Him and was transfigured before them: "His face shone like the sun, and his clothes became as white as the light" (Matthew 17:2). Then Jesus talked with Moses and Elijah.

Peter is the only disciple of the three who is recorded as speaking on top of that holy mountain. We hear him blurting out in verses 4–5:

> "Lord, it is good for us to be here. If you wish, I will put up three shelters—one for you, one for Moses and one for Elijah."
>
> While he was still speaking, a bright cloud covered them, and a voice from the cloud said, "This is my Son, whom I love; with him I am well pleased. Listen to him!"

God was telling Peter—who was growing in his faith journey and often putting his proverbial foot in his mouth—to be quiet and listen!

It is imperative that we do more listening than speaking if we are to grow in faith. Prayer (talking to God) is more listening than speaking.

Think about another well-known account: Peter getting out of the boat during a stormy night to walk on the water toward Jesus. We read in Matthew 14:25–31:

> Shortly before dawn Jesus went out to them, walking on the lake. When the disciples saw him walking on the lake, they were terrified. "It's a ghost," they said, and cried out in fear.
>
> But Jesus immediately said to them: "Take courage! It is I. Don't be afraid."
>
> "Lord, if it's you," Peter replied, "tell me to come to you on the water."
>
> "Come," he said.
>
> Then Peter got down out of the boat, walked on the water and came toward Jesus. But when he saw the wind, he was afraid and, beginning to sink, cried out, "Lord, save me!"
>
> Immediately Jesus reached out his hand and caught him. "You of little faith," he said, "why did you doubt?"

Notice, Peter was the only disciple to get out of the boat in the midst of a "contrary" wind (verse 24 NKJV) and walk on the water toward Jesus. None of the other disciples dared to try that faith adventure!

Oftentimes there is risk involved in our faith journey. The question we must ask ourselves is this: Am I going to trust God and step out in faith, or do I play it safe? The other disciples probably never even thought about stepping out of that safe environment and into the windy waves. They may even have thought, *There goes Peter again, doing something reckless.*

There will be times in your journey when well-meaning people close to you will question your sanity.

I vividly recall the time I felt like Peter getting out of the boat. I had just talked on the phone with that chaplain recruiter stationed at the Sixth U.S. Army Headquarters in the Presidio of San Francisco, which I wrote about in chapter 3. After I shared the conversation with Esther, I shocked her by saying that I believed God was calling us into the Army chaplaincy. This would mean a wholesale change in our lives, a move from Sacramento to the San Francisco Bay Area to attend seminary, and a host of other things. Actually, I think we were both in shock. It was a move that would affect the rest of our lives. God was leading, yet it required a step of faith.

We took that step.

U.S. founding father Thomas Jefferson said it best: "With great risk comes great reward."

Times come in all our lives when we are required to step out of our comfort zones into the unknown. If we want our faith to grow, we must put our full trust in God's plan and in His Word. We love our comfort zones and don't want to venture too far away from our peaceful places. But we must be willing to put it all on the line, like the pioneers of our faith over the millennia.

Putting It All on the Line

William Gurnall, a seventeenth-century English author and Puritan clergyman, believed that Christians need courage and determination if they hope to obey their "heavenly Captain's orders." Gurnall, the author of *The Christian in Complete Armour*, a classic on spiritual warfare, wrote:

> As part of Christ's army, you march in the ranks of gallant spirits. Every one of your fellow soldiers is the child of a King.

Some, like you, are in the midst of the battle, besieged on every side by affliction and temptation. Others, after many assaults, repulses, and rallyings of their faith, are already standing upon the wall of heaven as conquerors. From there they look down and urge you, their comrades on earth, to march up the hill after them. This is their cry: "Fight to the death and the City is your own, as now it is ours! For the waging of a few days' conflict, you will be rewarded with heaven's glory. One moment of this celestial joy will dry up all your tears, heal all your wounds, and erase the sharpness of the fight with the joy of your permanent victory."

In a word—God, angels, and the saints already with the Lord are spectators, watching how you conduct yourself as a child of the Most High. This crowd of witnesses (Hebrews 12:1) shouts joyfully from the celestial sidelines every time you defeat a temptation, scale a difficulty, or regain lost ground from your enemies. And if the fight should be too much for you, your dear Savior stands by with reserves for your relief at a moment's notice. . . . And when you come off the field, he will receive you joyously as the Father received Him upon His return to heaven. Would you be a valiant warrior?[4]

Such a valiant warrior was Desmond Thomas Doss, a private first class who was awarded the Medal of Honor in 1945 for his heroic action of saving the lives of 75 of his fellow servicemen during World War II.

Doss had been severely harassed by men in his own unit for refusing to carry a weapon, which was against his religious beliefs as a Seventh-day Adventist. His unit, in which he served as a combat medic, had been ordered to Okinawa to fight the Japanese, who were dug into the top of a nearly impenetrable four-hundred-foot-high escarpment known as Hacksaw Ridge (the title of Mel Gibson's 2016 biographical war film about Doss). The men had to use cargo nets to surmount the overhang near the top of the escarpment. All the while the Japanese were inflicting heavy causalities on Doss' unit.

Here is what happened, starting on May 2, 1945:

> Unarmed, Doss treated the wounded under enemy fire. He had removed any markings indicating he was medic, as Japanese forces knew taking out one medic could result in the loss of more GIs who would have no one to help them. Over the next several days, Doss continually put himself in mortal danger to aid his fallen comrades. Unafraid to rush into harm's way, he worked to save the very men who had once threatened his own life.
>
> By May 5, the fighting intensified to the point that all men were ordered to retreat. Doss refused. An estimated 75 men remained behind, too wounded to retreat under their own power. He would not leave them behind. Doss successfully rescued 75 men trapped at the top of the escarpment by lowering them with a special knot he knew. He had miraculously not been wounded and stayed in the fight with B Company.[5]

A few weeks later, Doss was wounded several times, but he insisted that others with more serious injuries be treated ahead of him.

Doss believed that God had assigned him to Okinawa so he could save the lives of those men and give glory to God. He was awarded the Medal of Honor, he said, simply because he followed the Golden Rule:[6] "In everything, do to others what you would have them do to you" (Matthew 7:12).

Is there anything more sacred than performing a mission that God has given you? Doss' faith that God had placed him there, and that saving those men was what God was asking him to do, gave him the confidence to perform heroically under intense pressure and danger.

It may be that God has not asked you to do such a feat, but the question remains, What is it that God has ordained you to do, for His glory?

In the next chapter we will look at some simple, practical ideas for where you can start your journey to accomplish the mission, plan and purpose God has for you.

STRATEGIC SPIRITUAL EXERCISES

1. What people, gifts and opportunities has God placed in your life to strengthen your faith in Him? How have those things strengthened your faith?

2. Read Matthew 14:25–31. What do you think made Peter decide to step out of the boat and walk on the water? Apply this story to your own life. Have you taken any faith challenges?

3. Reread the story of Enoch in Genesis 5:21–24. Are there ways Enoch's faith can encourage you?

4. What do you think gave Desmond Doss the courage to save those men's lives? Apply that to a challenge you are facing today.

8

PLANS AND PURPOSE

"What king, going to make war against another king, does not sit down first and consider whether he is able with ten thousand to meet him who comes against with twenty thousand?"

Luke 14:31 NKJV

Winter 1993. The Combat Maneuver Training Center (CMTC), Hohenfels, Germany. Early morning. "Chaplain Giammona, just how long do you think you can sustain your current pace of operations?" asked my observer controller.

"What do you mean, sir?" I asked.

"You've been running at a high rate of speed for days now, with little to no rest."

"Well, sir, I figure I can sustain my pace for as long as this exercise lasts."

"This exercise will last a few more days," returned my OC. "But can you sustain this kind of pace in actual combat over six months to a year?"

I saw his point, so I went back to the drawing board to plan a strategy that would work over the long haul.

Planning and strategy are two different things. Planning is the design or mechanism for how things would work—in my case, my new approach to ministry in combat over the long haul. It meant taking periodic breaks, getting needed rest, eating good and nutritious food, getting regular physical exercise and, most importantly, spending time alone with God. There would be times of intense stress in combat and taking care of soldiers—those who were wounded physically, emotionally and spiritually. But the important thing for me to learn was this: I could not care for them if I did not take care of myself.

Strategy, simply put, is making right choices. While planning is working out those choices or details, strategy is the ability to choose wisely which plans will accomplish your goal or objective according to the resources on hand or the resources you believe will be given to you by God. In terms of the above story, I chose to employ a long-term approach to my schedule that would sustain me over time (strategy), and then I planned accordingly.

Planning is the hallmark of military strategy. The Pentagon has a contingency plan for almost every possible conflict out there, both now and in the future. There are countless plans in vast data banks waiting to be dusted off and used. The purpose of those plans is to provide a well-thought-out foundation that can be tweaked for any particular course of action.

Jeremiah 29:11 says, "I know the thoughts that I think toward you, says the Lord, thoughts of peace and not of evil, to give you a future and a hope" (NKJV). Many today are asking, in light of the end times, "What kind of plans and purpose does God have for me?" And, even more importantly, "How do I find out those plans?"

Where to Begin

The plans and purposes of God are often revealed not all at once but unfurled like a flag over time. They are developed through our relationship with Him, just as an ever-deepening canyon is cut over time by the river flowing continually past the rock. God is more interested in you and your relationship with Him than in what you do for Him and His Kingdom. So as we talked about in the last chapter, it is important to be walking with Him every day and developing your ability to hear His voice.

From there, if you are to fulfill God's purpose and assignments for your life, you must master the art of planning and strategy. In real time, this looks hard to achieve, but it is walking and listening to God daily that is at the heart of godly plans and strategy.

For instance, if my overall strategy in life is to hear the Lord say to me when I am welcomed in the Kingdom, "Well done, good and faithful servant!" (Matthew 25:21), then I must "work out [my] salvation with fear and trembling," according to Philippians 2:12. I achieve this by being a devoted follower of Christ. The plan includes intentionality with daily Bible reading and study, dedicated prayer time, attendance at church that helps me grow as a disciple, weekly fellowship with other believers, focusing on the important aspects of life and more.

The most important word in this chapter—and maybe in this book—is *simplicity*. Nobody can plan an overly complex strategy and execute it successfully. An article from Columbia Business School, quoting Prussian General Carl von Clausewitz, says:

> A strategy must be distilled into the simplest language possible so that everyone in an organization can follow it. Complexity

paralyzes. Simplicity empowers. Simplicity is not a short cut; it's hard work — requiring the kind of intense mental engagement Clausewitz emphasizes.[1]

The apostle Paul told the church at Corinth, "I fear, lest somehow, as the serpent deceived Eve by his craftiness, so your minds may be corrupted from the simplicity that is in Christ" (2 Corinthians 11:3 NKJV). Simplicity is the straightforward, single-minded intent of your heart, mind and soul to accomplish the mission God has given you.

Following are some simple, practical ideas for how to continue your journey.

Your Spiritual Life

All things start with our relationship with Jesus Christ. Prayer, talking with God, is the key. Start and end your day with prayer, and continue to pray about everything throughout the day. My own practice is to get up every day and play Christian "soaking" instrumental prayer music off the internet while I pray.

Jesus taught His disciples how to pray by starting off with "Our Father, which art in heaven, hallowed be Thy name," indicating that praising our heavenly Father is the right way to start praying.

And seeking His face throughout the day is of utmost importance. God is pleased when we worship Him. "Seek the LORD and his strength, seek his face continually" (1 Chronicles 16:11 KJV).

During the day, continue in His presence. Talk to Him about what you are facing, whether it is at home, in the office, at the construction site, at school, in the hospital or wherever you are. Consider 1 Thessalonians 5:16–17 (NKJV): "Rejoice always. Pray without ceasing."

Before you go to sleep, review your day with Him. Let Him show you your strengths and weaknesses. Learn from Him what you should or should not have done. Praise Him for all things. Ask Him to reveal the mighty things He has planned for you: "Call to Me, and I will answer you, and show you great and mighty things, which you do not know" (Jeremiah 33:3 NKJV).

Read and study God's Word every day. There are plenty of read-through-the-Bible-in-a-year apps. Get one and use it. "Be diligent to present yourself approved to God, a worker who does not need to be ashamed, rightly dividing the word of truth" (2 Timothy 2:15 NKJV).

If you are married, read and pray with your spouse daily.

Your Physical Life

We often neglect the physical side of our lives, thinking that is not as important as the spiritual. But God has created us body, soul and spirit: "May your whole spirit, soul and body be kept blameless at the coming of our Lord Jesus Christ" (1 Thessalonians 5:23). Remember, Jesus became a man, a human being, to redeem us, the whole person. Our salvation includes the resurrection of our bodies.

In the first and second centuries, the heresy of Gnosticism taught that matter is evil and that freedom from the body comes through secret, exclusive knowledge. Some of the New Testament epistles resisted this growing heresy. The fact is, our bodies were created by God, and we are to be good stewards.

The best diet is no diet. Start now! Eat as much non-processed, organically grown fruit, vegetables, whole grains, fish and lean meat as possible. Cook at home so you know what is in your food. Stay away from soft drinks; sugar is a weight-gainer and a killer. In the U.S. alone, where more than two in five adults (42.4 percent) are obese,[2] the weight loss industry is worth $72.6 billion.[3] Fad diets are the face of much of this industry, and they have their followers buy processed foods that are not nutritionally healthy.

Exercise: Just do it! See your doctor before starting any exercise program. Be sensible. If you hardly ever exercise or have not done so in a long time, start slowly. Maybe take a short walk at first and then gradually build up. Try biking, swimming, gardening or hiking. Anything that gets your body moving and increases your blood flow is good. God made our bodies in such a way that they need physical exercise. Jesus Himself was in excellent physical condition; He continually walked many miles as He made His way around the towns and villages of Israel. Exercise will make you feel good. The important thing is consistency and regularity. Try for three to five times a week.

Your Intellectual Life

Cultivate healthy emotional and cognitive habits. Romans 12:2 says:

> Do not conform to the pattern of this world, but be transformed by the renewing of your mind. Then you will be able to test and approve what God's will is—his good, pleasing, and perfect will.

This means, in part, to turn off that soap opera, the so-called comedy show or the filth coming out of much of the media today in whatever form it takes, including social media. Not all television and media are bad, but most of it today is not helpful. There are, on the other hand, many Christian media platforms that will uplift and entertain you. Check them out.

Education is important—the *right* education, that is. Much of what is taught in higher education is progressive, socialist or even Communist in perspective. Attend a reputable Christian college or university, or go to a trade school to learn a focused profession such as avionics, culinary arts or mechanics.

Reading or listening to great books and audiobooks is a worthwhile pastime. Enlarge your library and discover the difference it can make in your life. It has been shown that many great leaders have awesome libraries in their homes. If this isn't feasible, visit your local library and borrow books and videos that can improve your mind, help you learn a new skill or craft, enlighten your intellect and improve your vocabulary.

Church is a great place not only to worship the Lord but to fellowship with other believers, get involved in a Bible study, help the needy and even go abroad on mission trips. All these are good for your health!

Power from on High

Many make the mistake of planning and then asking God to bless their plans. But the God factor is the most important element in all your plans and strategies. Find out what He is up to, and then ask Him if you can join Him in His plans for your life. If you do not do this, you will experience times when, although you are doing the best you know how, things are simply not working out.

The Bible tells the fascinating story of the king of Aram planning for war against Israel. He was conferring with his officers and laying out plans to defeat God's people. But his plans kept being thwarted, and he thought there must be a spy in his court. He did not know that Elisha, the man of God in Israel, was hearing directly from God and then revealing Aram's war plans to Israel's king.

> After conferring with his officers, [the king of Aram] said, "I will set up my camp in such and such a place."

The man of God sent word to the king of Israel: "Beware of passing that place, because the Arameans are going down there." So the king of Israel checked on the place indicated by the man of God. Time and again Elisha warned the king, so that he was on his guard in such places.

This enraged the king of Aram. He summoned his officers and demanded of them, "Tell me! Which of us is on the side of the king of Israel?"

"None of us, my lord the king," said one of his officers, "but Elisha, the prophet who is in Israel, tells the king of Israel the very words you speak in your bedroom."

2 Kings 6:8–12

The irate king ordered his officers to capture Elisha, but the prophet—God's top-secret espionage weapon—was under God's protection and perfectly safe. It never goes well to fight against God's people, purpose and program.

You have access to the very same weapon that was active more than 2,800 years ago in the prophet Elisha. That weapon is called the Holy Spirit.

Most believers focus on the Father and the Son, but we must remember the third Person of the Trinity, the Holy Spirit, who leads us into all truth. He can reveal things hidden in your life and in the lives of others, and He wants to reveal God's plans and purposes for you. Jesus told His disciples that "the Helper, the Holy Spirit whom the Father will send in My name, He will teach you all things, and remind you of all that I said to you" (John 14:26 NASB). The Holy Spirit is our Guide, our Helper and our Comforter in this life.

The Holy Spirit not only reveals the truth, as He did with Elisha, but He empowers us:

When the day of Pentecost came, they were all together in one place. Suddenly a sound like the blowing of a violent wind came

118

from heaven and filled the whole house where they were sitting. They saw what seemed to be tongues of fire that separated and came to rest on each of them. All of them were filled with the Holy Spirit and began to speak in other tongues as the Spirit enabled them.

Acts 2:1–4

Some mistakenly teach that the experience of being filled with the Holy Spirit was only for the first century. But the truth is that we, too, can be filled with the Holy Spirit. Others teach that when we are saved, we receive the Holy Spirit at that time. While that is true, we see that Peter and John laid hands on the people of Samaria to receive the Holy Spirit when they were already saved:

Now when the apostles who were at Jerusalem heard that Samaria had received the word of God, they sent Peter and John to them, who, when they had come down, prayed for them that they might receive the Holy Spirit. For as yet He had fallen upon none of them. They had only been baptized in the name of the Lord Jesus. Then they laid hands on them, and they received the Holy Spirit.

Acts 8:14–17 NKJV

Throughout the entire book of Acts, we read about the baptism and work of the Holy Spirit. His work has not stopped for the last two thousand years, and it will continue until the return of Christ and beyond.

Charles G. Finney, one of America's most powerful evangelists, president of Oberlin College and leader in the Second Great Awakening, wrote about this work of the Spirit:

The Apostles and brethren, on the Day of Pentecost, received it. What did they receive? What power did they exercise after that event?

They received a powerful baptism of the Holy Ghost, a vast increase of divine illumination. This baptism imparted a great diversity of gifts that were used for the accomplishment of their work. It manifestly included the following things: The power of a holy life. The power of a self-sacrificing life . . . The power of a cross-bearing life. The power of great meekness, which this baptism enabled them everywhere to exhibit. The power of a loving enthusiasm in proclaiming the gospel. The power of teaching. The power of a loving and living faith. The gift of inspiration, or the revelation of many truths before unrecognized by them. The power of moral courage to proclaim the gospel and do the bidding of Christ, whatever it might cost them.[4]

Your own mission, plan and strategy in life will never be fulfilled without the Holy Spirit guiding you and without His power working in you. We will talk more about this in chapter 11.

STRATEGIC SPIRITUAL EXERCISES

1. Reread the section titled "Where to Begin" and start to put into practice the spiritual, physical and intellectual habits listed there.
2. Reread 2 Kings 6:8–12, and then read the rest of the story in verses 9–23. What do you see in this story that you can apply to your life?
3. Begin to study the book of Acts, paying particular attention to the activity of the Holy Spirit.
4. Seek out those you know who are used by God. Ask them what "secrets" make them effective servants for Him.
5. Ask the Lord to help you begin to lay out a strategy and plan for your life from here on. Show it to others in whom you trust. Get their reaction.

9

FAITH AND FRICTION

Faith and friction are a big part of life, without which we would be spiritual infants who never grow up in God.

Colonel David J. Giammona

Summer 1986. Fort Jackson, South Carolina. My Army Reserve battalion under the 91st Division at the Presidio of San Francisco had been ordered to deploy to Fort Jackson for our annual two-week active-duty training (ADT). Prior to our deployment, my brigade chaplain directed me to go to the military clothing sale at the Presidio and purchase my first set of Army uniforms (known as the battle dress uniform / BDU), along with boots, belt, T-shirt, insignias and everything needed so I would look like an officer.

I had not even been to the chaplain basic course, and I was so new to the Army that I had to be shown how to wear the uniform. But I was commissioned as a second lieutenant chaplain candidate by direct Presidential appointment, meaning I could wear the uniform immediately.

When we arrived at Fort Jackson, I was directed to go with a sergeant first class (E7) to the military clothing store to get the uniforms cleaned and pressed. We traveled by military van to the store. I remember what happened next as if it were yesterday.

As the sergeant and I were standing in line, a mean-looking Army colonel came crashing through the front door, yelling at the top of his lungs, asking who had parked an unauthorized military van outside the store.

I foolishly raised my hand to indicate I was responsible, while the E7 stood right behind me, straight as an arrow, almost invisible. The colonel raced up to me and gave me a scolding I will never forget. Evidently it was forbidden at Fort Jackson to use military vehicles to go to the military clothing store.

Man, I thought, *this is my first day on the job in the Army, and it looks like it'll be my last.*

After my berating, and after the E7 and I did what we came to do, I made a beeline back to my unit to report to my brigade chaplain what had happened. Evidently, as we later found out, that colonel had not been selected for promotion to brigadier general and was lashing out. I had been the unfortunate victim.

Through the years of my experience in the Army, I learned that friction, both in training and in war, was a nearly daily occurrence.

One of the best-known generals of World War II, George S. Patton, was a tough disciplinarian and hot-tempered warrior who played life with reckless abandon. Those factors and many more made him one of the greatest generals in U.S. history. It also made him a feared commander by the German and American forces alike. It likewise got him into hot water on numerous occasions.

One famous story about Patton came about when, fresh from his triumph at Palermo, Italy, in August 1943, he visited a field hospital outside of Nicosia, and observed one soldier who did not seem to be wounded. When Patton found out the soldier was suffering from battle fatigue (now known as post-traumatic stress disorder or PTSD), he went into a rage, slapped the soldier in the face with his leather glove and kicked him out of the tent. It was later reported that the soldier had dysentery and a high fever.

A week later Patton had a similar encounter with another soldier.

These events were reported up the chain all the way to General Dwight D. Eisenhower, soon to become supreme Allied commander in Europe, and they eventually got leaked to the press. Many in Congress and the press called for Patton's head, and the U.S. Senate delayed his promotion to major general. This shocked Patton, who thought it was the end of the line for him. But Eisenhower could not afford to lose a military genius, so he reprimanded Patton and ordered him to apologize to the soldiers, allowing Patton to keep his job. Later Patton wanted to push on with his Third Army to Berlin, but Eisenhower rejected the idea, since the Yalta agreement had already allotted the city to the Soviets.[1]

Patton surely learned a few things along the way. The incidents with those two soldiers, according to *Encyclopaedia Britannica*, "likely cost him a command role of ground forces in the Normandy invasion in June 1944."[2]

Often the only way to learn is through friction and difficulty.

Not Shrinking from Issues

We experience friction on and off the field of battle. I saw it firsthand many times. Tempers often flare over seemingly insignificant things. When you are under the constant stress of war, things can go awry quickly. But it is the friction of war in the trenches that produces the best warriors and leaders. In fact, when high-ranking leaders are chosen, such as general officers, the military looks to see what actual combat those individuals have experienced over the years. They do not want non-combat leaders in charge of troops going to war.

Not only military leadership but faith is developed through friction. We wish it were not so, but as we read the Bible, we see that many of the greatest heroes of the faith were men and women who experienced profound difficulties. The faith of Abraham, Joseph, Moses, Deborah, David, Peter, Paul and many more was developed in the crucible of trouble.

Prussian General Carl von Clausewitz famously said:

> Friction is the only conception which, in a general way, corresponds to that which distinguishes real war from war on paper. The military machine, the army and all belonging to it, is in fact simple; and appears, on this account, easy to manage. But let us reflect that no part of it is in one piece, that it is composed entirely of individuals, each of which keeps up its own friction in all directions.[3]

Sooner or later, we are all tested in the crucible of life. Friction and faith go hand in hand. You cannot have one without the other.

Easy believe-ism says that since Jesus Christ already paid the price for our sins, we do not have to suffer or go through hard times. Jesus *did* pay the price. Many of His disciples, including James, Peter and Paul, and likely others, died as martyrs for their faith. One of His disciples, the apostle John, according to the theologian Tertullian, was plunged into oil by the Romans, but miraculously escaped. Only after that was he exiled to Patmos.

Eric Metaxas says that many of today's churches are preaching what Dietrich Bonhoeffer called cheap grace. Metaxas says:

Globalists and Marxists have taken over much of the Church, and everywhere you look, you see globalist, Marxist authoritarianism coming into America.

Listen, if it was about real evangelism in churches, I'd be all for it, but it's fake evangelism. In other words, you can get all these people "saved," and your church filled, but where is that church going to be ten years from now? Are those people going to be grounded in the faith? Are they going to be warriors for Christ willing to stand for the truth? Or are they going to be weak Christians who, the moment the wind blows this way or that, fall away?

We've already seen that. There are plenty of churches blowing whichever way the zeitgeist blows. They don't want to battle with anybody, so they'll go along with Black Lives Matter, critical race theory, transgender nonsense, the pride lobby and so on.

What we are facing in America is the cancellation of religious liberty. Soon it could be the cancellation of churches. If you don't see that we are called to stand—if you're nervous that somebody is going to say, "You're being political"—then essentially you're already dead.

This idea has become an idol in itself: "We can never touch on anything political." Which is complete nonsense. If you're talking about the slave trade in the seventeenth, eighteenth and nineteenth centuries, or if you're talking about abortion today, there are a million things that bring you into the political arena. Why should you shrink from that? It's not biblical to shrink from those issues just because somebody says, "Aha! You're being political."[4]

But many faith leaders and pastors today prefer to stick with evangelism, sharing the Good News of Jesus Christ and avoiding the implications of our faith. Metaxas comments:

That's a very safe path. We think we can just speak on the things that will draw people to Christ and avoid having to touch on any of this divisive stuff, all this culture war stuff or anything political. We want to be nice and winsome.

But I'm here to tell you that, at the end of the day, you can't do that. At some point God calls us to speak the truth. Some people can speak it more winsomely than others, but if you think you can just stick to evangelism, you're kidding yourself and avoiding God's call. Jesus did not do that. It's simply not biblical.

But a lot of pastors have made an idol of evangelism. They aren't worshiping the God of Scripture, who commands us to speak into these issues and to condemn corruption, bad ideas, wickedness and lying. That's part of what it means to be a Christian. But when discipleship goes out the window, we end up with very, very shallow Christians, who ultimately aren't Christians at all.[5]

Instead of *Letter to the American Church*, Metaxas originally considered calling his newest bestselling book *Faith without Works Is Dead* because, he says, that largely explains what is happening today:

There is this idea that we can act as though we just "believe" things in our heads, without having to live out our faith. I just need to "believe" and then I'm saved. But we have to ask, Do you *really* believe? If you're not acting on your faith, if the works aren't there, then the Lord is going to look at your life and say, "I don't see the evidence that you're saved. You say intellectually that you believe those things, but if you believe them, you're actually going to *live* as though you believe them. And I don't see the evidence that you're living that way." We cannot fool God.

So at the heart of this—which is also at the heart of how the Germans got it wrong—is the fundamental misconception that faith is just some intellectual assent to a few points of theology: "I believe Jesus rose from the dead. I believe He died for my sins." But in reality you have to live it, or you really have no faith, whatever you might think.[6]

In other words, we have to pay the price.

Let's look at what the Bible says about faith and friction:

Count it all joy, my brothers, when you meet trials of various kinds, for you know that the *testing of your faith* produces steadfastness. And let steadfastness have its full effect, that you may be perfect and complete, lacking in nothing.

James 1:2–4 ESV, emphasis added

Our faith is in the continual process of testing to see if it is genuine.

Lessons from the Crucible

If anyone in the Bible was tested, it was surely the biblical hero Abraham. God promised him that he would have a son, and that his descendants would be as numerous as the stars in the sky (see Genesis 15:5). But Abraham was already 75 years old, and he had to wait 25 years to see the promise fulfilled.

During this waiting period God tested him—and frankly, Abraham failed the test. His wife, Sarah, gave him Hagar, her maidservant, to be his wife, and she became pregnant. Abraham and Sarah's impatience to help God out, leading to the birth of Ishmael, caused a multitude of problems for Abraham and Sarah and Hagar—and for the Jews, God's chosen people, right up to the present day.

But God fulfilled His promise. Abraham's son Isaac, born when Abraham was one hundred and Sarah was ninety, was the promised heir to everything Abraham possessed, and the key to God's promise that Abraham would be "the father of many nations" (Genesis 17:4).

Then came the test. God told him,

> "Take your son, your only son Isaac, whom you love, and go to the land of Moriah, and offer him there as a burnt offering on one of the mountains of which I shall tell you."
>
> Genesis 22:2 ESV

Abraham was in a predicament. Isaac, the son he loved, was his promised heir. How could God have told him to kill him?

All of us would say that could not have been God. God does not contradict Himself. But God was testing Abraham's faith to see if he would follow His instructions.

Just as Abraham was raising the knife to kill his son, the Lord called him.

> "Do not lay your hand on the boy or do anything to him, for now I know that you fear God, seeing you have not withheld your son, your only son, from me." And Abraham lifted up his eyes and looked, and behold, behind him was a ram, caught in a thicket by his horns. And Abraham went and took the ram and offered it up as a burnt offering instead of his son.
>
> verses 12–13 ESV

Abraham knew, even in this most severe of trials, that if God had told him to do this, then God had a plan.

In the New Testament we read that Abraham was commended for his faith:

> By faith Abraham, when he was tested, offered up Isaac, and he who had received the promises was in the act of offering up his only son, of whom it was said, "Through Isaac shall your

offspring be named." He considered that God was able even to raise him from the dead, from which, figuratively speaking, he did receive him back.

Hebrews 11:17–19 esv

Abraham reckoned that if he put his son to death, God could raise him from the dead.

Please hear us. We are not saying that, in our day and age, anyone has the right to kill anyone else. There have been too many murders by people who said God told them to do it. No, the challenge to Abraham was a one-time command from God to test his faith and see if he would carry out the order. When it was obvious to God—and to Abraham—that he would, the Lord stopped him and provided a ram for the sacrifice.

It is interesting to note that Mount Moriah, according to some scholars, may be at or very near the hill of Golgotha, where God offered His own Son as a sacrifice for the sins of the world.

We can learn invaluable lessons from Abraham about having our own faith tested in the crucible. There will be times in our lives when we do not understand what is happening. God may have promised something but it has not come to pass. We want to take matters into our own hands, but we will make a mess of things.

It may be that God is testing us. It may be that the timing is not right. It may be that God has not yet worked out all the pieces.

Here is a truthful statement: Just because we do not see God working does not mean He is not. He may not be on our timetable or schedule, but He is working things out. Patience is not easy, but it is key.

God's Waiting Room

How do we hold on during the difficult times?

Mary Ann Peluso McGahan, a minister, conference speaker and Gospel music singer who worked closely with David Wilkerson at Times Square Church in New York City, says:

> The Lord takes us through trials, sicknesses, disappointments, betrayals, everything—to help build our faith and prepare us for the mission He's given us. So He gives a vision, an assignment, and then He goes silent—and it's for our character to grow, our integrity to grow, our faith to grow. And He keeps us in check so when that assignment or vision or ministry or business comes to fruition, it doesn't overtake us. That isn't the thing. The Lord remains the focus. He remains our first love.
>
> For me, it was six years of going through a lot of sickness. I had some hard times and disappointments. But through that, the Lord spoke to me and said, *Never let the work of the ministry become your lord.*[7]

At the time Peluso McGahan had been singing at major crusades and other events.

> But during that time, I found that nothing in this world compares to the Person of Jesus in my life—not even ministry. So I think God uses the hard times to develop our character, so that our character can meet up with our God-given vision, and it's not off balance. Not that we don't stop growing, but so we can handle the exposure and the trials that come with it.[8]

Peluso McGahan's story and Abraham's story reveal that control is an illusion. We think we are in control, but in reality we are not. We may have outlined a grand strategic plan for our lives, but Proverbs 16:9 states, "In their hearts humans plan their course, but the LORD establishes their steps." This does not mean we have no say in the plans or purposes of our lives, but we always look to God for both the origin and the outcome. He has the final say.

What about when we wait on God and nothing is happening? Pastor Rick Warren, founder of Saddleback Church in Lake Forest, California, talks about being "stuck in God's waiting room."[9]

While there is only one word in the English language for *wait*, there are many words in the Hebrew language; some scholars say there are more than twenty. One appears in the much-loved promise from Isaiah 40:31 (NKJV): "Those who wait on the LORD shall renew their strength; they shall mount up with wings like eagles, they shall run and not be weary, they shall walk and not faint."

One of the words for *wait* in Hebrew is *qavah*, meaning to look eagerly for; to gather in oneness; to be bound together. "Wait" does not mean to do nothing; it means to gather with other believers and draw from their strength in the earnest expectation of something great from God. Some translations use the word *hope*, but that is not the full meaning of the word.

What God asks of us does not always make sense to us. We must remember that He sees everything from the beginning to the end. He is looking at all of eternity, from the temporary perspective of our lives and from the eternal perspective of heaven and beyond. We are looking through a keyhole while God surveys the entire universe. As He says in Isaiah 66:1: "Heaven is my throne, and the earth is my footstool. Where is the house you will build for me? Where will my resting place be?"

Yes, there are times when we scratch our heads and wonder why God does what He does. But we must remember all the while that

"My thoughts are not your thoughts, neither are your ways my ways," declares the LORD. "As the heavens are higher than the

131

earth, so are my ways higher than your ways and my thoughts than your thoughts."

Isaiah 55:8–9

The military expects friction as a natural occurrence of war. The Bible also expects it. The apostle Peter wrote: "Dear friends, do not be surprised at the fiery ordeal that has come on you to test you, as though something strange were happening to you" (1 Peter 4:12). Friction is part of growing and growing up in the faith.

The apostle Paul is one of the greatest examples of a disciple of Jesus who went through hard times during his assignment from God. Once, when he compared himself to false apostles, he wrote:

I have worked harder, been put in prison more often, been whipped times without number, and faced death again and again. Five different times the Jewish leaders gave me thirty-nine lashes. Three times I was beaten with rods. Once I was stoned. Three times I was shipwrecked. Once I spent a whole night and a day adrift at sea. I have traveled on many long journeys. I have faced danger from rivers and from robbers. I have faced danger from my own people, the Jews, as well as from the Gentiles. I have faced danger in the cities, in the deserts, and on the seas. And I have faced danger from men who claim to be believers but are not. I have worked hard and long, enduring many sleepless nights. I have been hungry and thirsty and have often gone without food. I have shivered in the cold, without enough clothing to keep me warm.

2 Corinthians 11:23–27 NLT

Despite all this, as we saw in chapter 6, Paul kept his eye on the prize: "I press on toward the goal to win the prize for which God has called me heavenward in Christ Jesus" (Philippians 3:14).

Most believers in the West have not been called to go through what many followers of Jesus have gone through over the centuries and are going through now in various parts of the world. We must not expect, however, that following Jesus is always going to be a pleasant journey on a smooth road. Franklin Graham, president and CEO of the Billy Graham Evangelistic Association and Samaritan's Purse, told attendees at a National Religious Broadcasters convention in May 2023 to consider a world in which standing for God's Word might be against the law:

> Jesus told us the world hated [Him] first and they're going to hate you. If you stand for Christ, the world is going to hate you. I believe there's a coming storm that we're all going to [have to] be ready for. It's not going to be good. The world is deteriorating so quickly. It seems like every demon in hell has been turned loose.[10]

Regardless of what perils the future holds, however, we can take encouragement in the words of Jesus from the Sermon on the Mount:

> "Blessed are those who are persecuted for righteousness' sake, for theirs is the kingdom of heaven. Blessed are you when others revile you and persecute you and utter all kinds of evil against you falsely on my account. Rejoice and be glad, for your reward is great in heaven, for so they persecuted the prophets who were before you."
>
> Matthew 5:10–12 ESV

════ STRATEGIC SPIRITUAL EXERCISES ════

1. Reread the commendation of Abraham in Hebrews 11:17–19. What can you learn from his faith and sacrificial obedience?

2. Think about one or two of your favorite Bible characters. Did they go through hard knocks? How did they handle them?

3. Look up the life of General Patton and read about some incidents in his life when things did not go so well. What principles can you learn?

4. Discuss with someone you trust a painful experience from the past, and how you handled it. Then discuss a difficulty you are facing now.

PART 3

FUTURE STRATEGIES

10

A NEW PURPOSE

We are an army out to set other men free.

Colonel Joshua Chamberlain
in the movie *Gettysburg*

Summer 2011. Gettysburg National Military Park, Gettysburg, Pennsylvania. As part of the Army War College strategic education for Army officers, we toured the Gettysburg battlefield with a Ph.D. professor who was our tour guide.

I had read all about the Battle of Gettysburg, and especially the Little Round Top fight, which some scholars say was the turning point of the entire Civil War. But I never thought I would one day walk the battlefield with someone as knowledgeable as that professor from the War College at Carlisle Barracks, Pennsylvania, whose advanced degree was in the Battle of Gettysburg.

It is an emotional moment to stand where men died in battle in 1863 to save America. Colonel Joshua Chamberlain, who led his 20th Maine Infantry Regiment in one of the most famous counterattacks in the Civil War, stands out as one of the bravest of men in U.S. military history. His valor eventually earned him the Medal of Honor.

I was informed, inspired and sobered as I walked the ground where the battle of Little Round Top took place. It is a memory etched onto my soul, something I will carry the rest of my life. *Little did he know when he woke up that morning what awaited him*, I mused. This description of the battle is from the United States National Guard:

> After marching all day and night to reach Gettysburg, the regiment was ordered late in the afternoon of July 2 to occupy critical terrain between two hills, Big and Little Round Top. Chamberlain was ordered to hold this position on the extreme left flank of the Union line at all costs; if outflanked by the Confederates, the entire Union position would be in jeopardy.
>
> It was not long before the 15th and 47th Alabama Regiments attacked. The 20th Maine held off six attacks by the determined Alabama men, but Colonel Chamberlain knew that his regiment, low on ammunition, could not withstand a seventh. He therefore ordered a counterattack with fixed bayonets, and the 20th charged down the slopes of Little Round Top into the startled Confederates and broke their attack. The 20th Maine took 400 prisoners and stopped the Confederate threat to the Union flank.[1]

I was awed to have walked the ground where the battle of Little Round Top took place. Colonel Chamberlain is one of my heroes in military history. His bold, decisive action on that fateful day, July 2, 1863, was pivotal. If the Confederate Army had gotten around his flank, it could have meant the defeat of the Union Army, and possibly the nation as we know it. Scholars debate this point, but one thing is clear: What Chamberlain did that day would live on in military history.

More than sixteen hundred casualties resulted from that one battle.[2] Men bled and died on that patch of ground. They had a purpose.

Made in God's Image

Everyone on planet earth is looking for purpose, whether they know it or not. The very definition of purpose means intent or intentionality—the reason something or someone exists. In other words, why am I here on earth and what am I supposed to do?

In the developing world, most people do not have the luxury of asking these questions; yet they remain in the very center of every being God has created.

To find our purpose, we must go back to the very beginning:

> Then God said, "Let us make mankind in our image, in our likeness, so that they may rule over the fish in the sea and the birds in the sky, over the livestock and all the wild animals, and over all the creatures that move along the ground." So, God created mankind in his own image, in the image of God he created them; male and female he created them.
>
> Genesis 1:26–27

The Latin phrase *imago Dei*, "image of God," refers to the creation of mankind in the image or likeness of God. Scholars for centuries have argued over the meaning of this phrase. How did God make us in His image? What does that even mean?

Human beings have some of the attributes or qualities of God that make us unique in all the universe. Here are four ways we were made in His image.

We Were Given Dominion

Being made in the image of God does not mean we are God. We will never be God! But we are unique—not on a par with the animals, contrary to what evolutionists say. God placed us above the rest of creation, to rule and have authority over it:

> God blessed [Adam and Eve] and said to them, "Be fruitful and increase in number; fill the earth and subdue it. Rule over the fish in the sea and the birds in the sky and over every living creature that moves on the ground."
>
> Genesis 1:28

At the Fall, when Adam and Eve disobeyed God and fell into sin, they lost dominion—but it was restored through the incarnation, death and resurrection of Jesus Christ, to whom it rightfully belongs: "All authority in heaven and on earth has been given to me" (Matthew 28:18).

But Jesus turned right around and delegated His authority to the Church: "I have given you authority to trample on snakes and scorpions and to overcome all the power of the enemy; nothing will harm you" (Luke 10:19). Now it is the believer's responsibility to take the authority given to us by the Lord Jesus Christ and use His name, His Word and the power of His Spirit to destroy every evil work that comes against our lives.

We Are Triune

God is triune—Father, Son and Holy Spirit—and He also created us triune (as we saw in chapter 8). The three elements that make up man's total nature or being are body, soul and spirit.

We Are Relational

God created us with the capacity for personal fellowship with Him and with each other. In Mark 12:29–31 we find the essence of this relational capacity when Jesus responded to a teacher of the law, who asked Him the most important commandment.

> "The most important one," answered Jesus, "is this: 'Hear, O Israel: The Lord our God, the Lord is one. Love the Lord your God with all your heart and with all your soul and with all your mind and with all your strength.' The second is this: 'Love your neighbor as yourself.' There is no commandment greater than these."

We Are Immortal

God is immortal since He has no beginning and no end. Mankind has a beginning but no end. You may ask, What about death? Doesn't life end in death? The answer is a resounding no! In death we transition to either life everlasting in heaven or to eternal destruction in hell.

Jesus told the Sadducees, who did not believe in a resurrection: "Even Moses showed that the dead rise, for he calls the Lord 'the God of Abraham, and the God of Isaac, and the God of Jacob.' He is not the God of the dead, but of the living, for to him all are alive" (Luke 20:38). And Jesus told the religious leaders, "I give [my sheep] eternal life, and they shall never perish" (John 10:28).

After the Fall

Tragically sin marred all that God created. At the Fall, everything good that God intended for mankind died. Adam and Eve did not die immediately in the sense of physical death, but the process of death and decay started right away, and sin now separated them from God. No longer did they rule over this planet. That was turned over to Satan.

The Bible calls Satan "the god of this world" (2 Corinthians 4:4 ESV). The world became a broken place. Relationships were ruined, sin held sway and the world turned dark. No longer did Adam and Eve possess the light they once had. Some scholars believe that Adam and Eve had been clothed or covered in light, reflecting the light of God's glory, but at the Fall, that light turned off. In any event, they now knew they were naked:

> They heard the sound of the LORD God walking in the garden in the cool of the day, and the man and his wife hid themselves from the presence of the Lord God among the trees of the garden. But the LORD God called to the man and said to him, "Where are you?" And he said, "I heard the sound of you in the garden, and I was afraid, because I was naked, and I hid myself." He said, "Who told you that you were naked? Have you eaten of the tree of which I commanded you not to eat?"
>
> Genesis 3:8–11 ESV

The good news is that Christ came to restore all things to Himself. The Gospel ("good news"!) is about the complete restoration of all things: the reconciliation of mankind to God; the renewal of planet earth; and the reestablishment of mankind to rule:

> Do you not know that the Lord's people will judge the world? And if you are to judge the world, are you not competent to judge trivial cases? Do you not know that we will judge angels? How much more the things of this life!
>
> 1 Corinthians 6:2–3

Coming around full circle, then, knowing that we are created in God's image, what is our purpose? To reflect the light of God to a lost and dying world in everything we do and say. The relationship with God once broken, and the light of His glory once lost, are now restored to us by Jesus' death on the cross. He paid the price for our sin so we can have restored fellowship with God and with each other. We now have the light of God reflected in our very beings.

So let your light shine in our dark world and bring many sons and daughters to God through our Lord Jesus Christ.

Moving Forward with Purpose

This purpose is the gas in our tank that propels us forward like nothing else.

Soldiers always want to know the reason for their mission, for without purpose there is no motivation to move into harm's way. It is the same for the believer. Lethargy and lack of purpose, says retired U.S. Army Chaplain (Colonel) Peter Brzezinski,

> often result from forgetting that God leads us step by step through life. Often we think of the grand picture and God's big plan for our lives. In this regard, it's important to understand your mission and your vision.
>
> Any commander will do that with his or her immediate military team, and say, "Our mission is to accomplish A, B and C. And our vision when it's done? This is what we want it to look like." That is the driving force and impulse that keep a military team on track and not get distracted with side things that can drift them off their mission and end up getting different results.[3]

So it is with believers, says Brzezinski, as we seek to find our place in God's army:

> You have to keep clearly in mind, "What's my mission? What's my vision?" A few of us take time to sit down and write it out,

think it out, and get people around us we can trust, because Scripture says in a multitude of counselors there is safety. God also works in step with our talents, our abilities, our gifts, our interests.

Many times He will exercise your faith muscles and put you in places and situations where you have to step up and take responsibility. You may feel like Moses: "Oh, I don't know. I can't. I'm not ready."

No, no, no! I had a commander in one unit, a lieutenant colonel when I was a captain, who said to me very clearly, "It's time for you to take over this mission, Captain." I responded, 'Well, I need to get this and that.' He said, 'Nope, you've got to do it today.'"[4]

Well, Brzezinski did it—not without some concern or even fear on his part—and the Lord blessed it. He wraps up:

We learn quickly in the military, and in many settings in life, that courage is not the absence of fear, but acting in the presence of it. I'm sure Moses was trembling when God said, "I need you to do this." And he said, "But, but, but . . ." That happens to us frequently as we seek the next thing in life that God has for us.

I think also that if we're going to grow and thrive in any particular calling or direction, opportunities will come to us through people, through instincts, through inclinations, through our own vision.

As you're looking at things and praying about them, the Lord will direct you. Not always in the time you think—sometimes more quickly, sometimes longer—but He has genuinely equipped you to do that work; otherwise you wouldn't have that interest.[5]

In Christ we have sublime meaning and purpose for life now and the life to come. Our faith journey is now and forever. It is wonderful to read the following Scripture and realize that the present age is not our entire purpose, and that we will be rewarded in the future heavenly Kingdom for our faithfulness now:

> By faith Abraham, when called to go to a place he would later receive as his inheritance, obeyed and went, even though he did not know where he was going. By faith he made his home in the promised land like a stranger in a foreign country; he lived in tents, as did Isaac and Jacob, who were heirs with him of the same promise. For he was looking forward to the city with foundations, whose architect and builder is God.
>
> Hebrews 11:8–10

Our Role in God's Army

In February 2023 a Holy Spirit outpouring began at Asbury University in Wilmore, Kentucky, that spread to churches and universities nationwide. During the same month, the film *Jesus Revolution* released. Based on a book of the same name by Greg Laurie, senior pastor of Harvest Christian Fellowship in Riverside, California, the film depicted the Jesus people movement of the late 1960s and early '70s in which hundreds of thousands of young people, including many hippies, came to faith in Jesus.

The revival and film brought hope to millions during a time when the world was experiencing the growing threat of nuclear war, the possibility of economic collapse, and widespread immorality and lawlessness. Says Pastor Paul Pickern, founder of All Pro Pastors International:

> It wasn't a coincidence that *Jesus Revolution,* in the making for a few years, was released during the strength of the Asbury revival. This is a revival among young people that many did not anticipate.

That's the beauty of my bird's-eye view of the Body of Christ with all these different denominations and cultures. As we see with these two things—the Asbury revival and *Jesus Revolution*—the revival doesn't care about denominations or color or culture or anything. It's just God at work, and you can either join in or be left behind. It's an exciting time to be part of God's army!

Another movie came out two weeks or so before the Asbury revival, *Left Behind: Rise of the Antichrist* with actor Kevin Sorbo. That wasn't by accident![6]

Given the encouraging timing of these events, it is especially important to understand our role in God's army so we can walk by faith in our assigned tasks, buoyed by the miraculous power of the Holy Spirit. Explains Pickern:

We are the voice of hope and victory. When you know who you are in Christ, you have no fear. That is where I truly see pastors and leaders speaking that not only *can* we win, but we *are* winning! We're walking in the power of the Holy Spirit, which is not just something that came two thousand years ago but is still happening today.

Praise God, we have young people in revival. And I'm seeing senior adults being led by the move of young people. Just a few months ago, I was part of a baptism where seventeen people were baptized, and the average age was 65.[7]

Pickern communicates regularly with hundreds of pastors and faith leaders worldwide. He says:

God is moving today like you would not believe. There are miracles, signs and wonders. God is raising people from the dead! He is making leprosy drop off people. Disabled people are walking. Men and women of God who know who they are— they're walking in faith and victory. People's lives are changing.

146

One of the greatest movements of God is going on in Iran today—a mighty move. It's incredible! And God is moving in some of the darkest places on earth. You see the joy of the Lord on somebody who is starving, and God is sustaining them. It gets back to this: "God, I need You, I love You, I praise You." God inhabits the praises of His people.

My prayer is that the revival happening will grow and that we will embrace it. We need to come together as God's army and realize, as Jesus said, that we are all different parts of this wonderful body called the Body of Christ. Praise God, we can love one another and reach the world for Christ.[8]

God's plan and purpose is to reconcile the world to Himself. What He created will be fully restored. Nothing He has made will be "subjected to futility" forever (Romans 8:20 NKJV). God's plans, although delayed, will not be stopped by any being in the universe. The earth and all of God's creation will find complete restoration in Christ.

Then He who sat on the throne said, "Behold, I make all things new." And He said to me, "Write, for these words are true and faithful." And He said to me, "It is done! I am the Alpha and the Omega, the Beginning and the End. I will give of the fountain of the water of life freely to him who thirsts. He who overcomes shall inherit all things, and I will be his God and he shall be My son."

Revelation 21:5–7 NKJV

═══ STRATEGIC SPIRITUAL EXERCISES ═══

1. What insights have you discovered about yourself after reading this chapter?

2. Read Genesis 1–3 and jot down notes about the problems that occurred as a result of the Fall, and the God-given purpose of men and women.

3. How are you moving forward into God's purpose? Begin today living out your new purpose in life by reflecting and expressing God's love and life to those around you.

4. Pray for an opportunity this week to share the light and love of Jesus with a friend, neighbor or someone you do not know.

11

GROWING IN FAITH
AND YOUR ASSIGNMENT

It's our turn now. That phrase kept repeating in my heart. It was
a clue of some kind. The feeling kept growing within that I would
witness some great event. Then the scales fell off my eyes. I real-
ized that as glorious as our tent crusades are, they are only a small
part of a great and widespread phenomenon brewing nationwide.
That is why I believe there is an urgent warning from the throne
of God to get ready for harvest.

Evangelist Mario Murillo, *It's Our Turn Now*

Winter 2005. Camp Arifjan, Kuwait. A high-ranking enlisted soldier steps
up to the platform in the multi-use facility, which seats around
seven hundred soldiers, and briefs us on the new Army cam-
ouflage uniform (ACU) soon to be distributed to the entire U.S.
Army worldwide.

This new combat uniform, he tells us, can be worn in urban
warfare zones as well as other areas of the world where we

will fight, including the deserts of the Middle East. He extols all the virtues of the uniform—to the point of being almost unbelievable.

So I talk with him backstage for a few moments and ask him jokingly if he believes all the rhetoric he just told us.

He laughs. "Nah, Chaplain, but I have to toe the party line."

In my 32-year stint with the Army, I saw numerous changes, not only of the uniform but of almost everything else.

Transformation is a word I heard almost every day. We were always transforming something, whether it was uniforms, tactics, equipment, training or whatever. The reason was simple: You either adapt or die. You cannot fight new wars using tactics or techniques of the last century.

That was proven in the Civil War, World War I and beyond. Rushing headlong in formation against the machine gun produced catastrophic results. Thousands died because the military refused to change. History expert Martin Kelly writes:

World War I saw a change in warfare, from the hand-to-hand style of older wars to the inclusion of weapons that used technology and removed the individual from close combat. The war had extremely high casualties, over 15 million dead and 20 million injured. The face of warfare would never be the same again.[1]

In the First Battle of the Marne in September 1914, the British and French armies fought the Germans in vicious trench warfare, when whole units would pour over their trenches and run toward the enemy, who was dug in with machine gun emplacements and artillery. With more than two million soldiers fighting this battle, as many as five hundred thousand were killed or wounded in action. Why?

Because they did not transform their thinking, their tactics or their strategy. They were using old Napoleonic methods from the late 1700s and early 1800s, when machine guns and modern artillery had not yet been invented. In the end, an estimated fifteen million soldiers were killed and twenty million wounded in World War I. The fighting had to end because there were no more young men to send to war.

A Time of Spiritual Transformation

The need for transformation is the same today in our lives and in the Church. We are either growing and being transformed in our faith or we are not. We will never accomplish our mission or purpose without daily spiritual transformation. We have already noted Romans 12:2:

> Do not conform to the pattern of this world, but be transformed by the renewing of your mind. Then you will be able to test and approve what God's will is—his good, pleasing, and perfect will.

Transformation and the renewing of the mind is an everyday process of growing in your faith, not only by reading the Bible, but by prayer and meditation in solitude, by reading books designed for spiritual health and growth, by listening to transformative sermons, by being committed to church and small fellowship groups, by being mentored by spiritually mature believers, by taking part in spiritual growth conferences and many other such wonderful habits.

Many churchgoers have a one-time experience with the Lord and little to nothing after that. Whole denominations are failing, not only because they are caught up in worldly thinking and practices (as we have seen), but because they are stuck in the past, relying on their history, caught up in legalism and not seeking the fresh anointing and power of the Holy Spirit. But our relationship with the Lord is not a static, one-time commitment; it is an ongoing, progressive, everyday journey with the living God.

Jesus had compassion on the poor, sick and needy, but He had little tolerance for the static religious leaders of his day. Here is how he described them:

> "The teachers of the law and the Pharisees sit in Moses' seat. So you must be careful to do everything they tell you. But do not do what they do, for they do not practice what they preach. They tie up heavy, cumbersome loads and put them on other people's shoulders, but they themselves are not willing to lift a finger to move them."
>
> Matthew 23:1–4

And Jesus had much more to say in censuring the religious leaders.

The legalism that characterized the teachers of the Law and the Pharisees is no different than what we can fall into ourselves. They got stuck in a form of religion that denied the power of God. Paul, a former Pharisee himself, warned his protégé Timothy about this:

> Know this, that in the last days perilous times will come: For men will be lovers of themselves, lovers of money, boasters, proud, blasphemers, disobedient to parents, unthankful, unholy, unloving, unforgiving, slanderers, without self-control, brutal, despisers of good, traitors, headstrong, haughty, lovers of pleasure rather than lovers of God, having a form of godliness but denying its power. And from such people turn away!
>
> 2 Timothy 3:1–5 NKJV

Who were the teachers of the Law (or scribes) and Pharisees, and how did they become so involved in the minutiae of the Law?

When the Second Temple (later known as Herod's Temple) was built in Jerusalem, after Solomon's Temple was destroyed by the Babylonians, a group of Jewish priests and scholars got together and determined to study, keep and abide by the Torah (or Law) so the Temple would never again be destroyed for neglect of God's commands and ordinances. This group became known as the Pharisees—strict legalists who adhered to the letter of the Law. They argued among themselves continually about what constituted the right interpretation of the Torah and its 613 legal commands (although this number is disputed by rabbinic lawyers). Although their intentions were good, they devolved into a hierarchical class of religious leaders over and above the ordinary Jews of Jesus' day.[2]

They spent their lives teaching every detail of the Law, as this article at Christianity.com attests:

> A perfect illustration is seen in the simple Sabbath law. The Bible clearly told the Israelite, "Do not work, do not bear burdens, but rest and keep it a holy day."
>
> Well, work had to be defined; carrying burdens had to be defined. For example, one could
>
> • get milk enough for one swallow, and
> • carry a spoon weighing no more than one fig.
>
> It was the scribes and Pharisees who were embroiled over the discussion as to whether, on the Sabbath, a woman could wear a brooch, a mother could pick up her child, or a man could wear his wooden leg. These were burdens.[3]

Jesus overturned the legalism of the religious leaders. He even upset their religious merchandising scheme:

On reaching Jerusalem, Jesus entered the temple courts and began driving out those who were buying and selling there. He overturned the tables of the money changers and the benches of those selling doves, and would not allow anyone to carry merchandise through the temple courts. And as he taught them, he said, "Is it not written: 'My house will be called a house of prayer for all nations'? But you have made it 'a den of robbers.'"

The chief priests and the teachers of the law heard this and began looking for a way to kill him, for they feared him, because the whole crowd was amazed at his teaching.

Mark 11:15–18

Notice that the very leaders Jesus confronted planned to kill him because they feared losing their positions of power, prestige and privilege. Their positions were more important to them than honoring God and His house.

When pastors and faith leaders are more worried about their "ministry" than their relationship with God, it is time to repent. The scribes and Pharisees devolved into a mess of religious corruption slowly over the process of years. Time will erode our faith, too, if we are not diligent in developing our walk day in and day out.

Last Call

In the previous chapter we talked about an outpouring of the Holy Spirit that started at Asbury University in Wilmore, Kentucky, in early 2023, which spread to colleges and other venues across the country.

Author and evangelist Anne Graham Lotz, daughter of world-renowned evangelist Billy Graham, commented on a text she received from her husband's nephew, Dr. John-Paul Lotz, who observed the revival in Kentucky firsthand:

Could what John-Paul observed be the beginning of the "latter rain"? An outpouring of God's Spirit in one last great awakening before Jesus returns? Lord God, let it be so . . . for the glory of Your great name, for the salvation of our nation, for the revival of Your people.[4]

Our hope and prayer are the same—that this outpouring will usher in the last worldwide great awakening, culminating with the return of Christ.

Mary Ann Peluso McGahan, minister, conference speaker and Gospel music singer, says she believes "the Holy Spirit is putting out one last call":

It's like the story Jesus told in Luke 15 about the king who put on a great feast and invited those of his household to come and feast with him. Many of them were busy, so he said to his servant, "Go out into the highways and byways and compel them to come in." I think we are in that hour, and there is one last call for those of us who have known the Lord to be revived, to be re-fired, to be more committed, to come into a place of intimacy with Him.

When I got saved in 1980, God brought me out of Hollywood and rock and roll. I was raking leaves in my mom's yard one day. I was poking underneath a chain-link fence to get out each leaf, taking my time because I love detail and organization. Then I looked up and noticed that it was getting dark. I had to get this done! So I began to take wide sweeps with the rake to get as many leaves as I could before it got dark.

Then the Holy Spirit said, *One last, great revival is coming, and then you're out of here*. It was like Joel 2, which Peter quoted on the Day of Pentecost: "In the last days I will pour out My Spirit." We are in the last of the last days.

Looking up the street, I saw in the Spirit people walking along the sidewalk. No one was around them. I saw one man fall on his face and cry out and repent. It was as if the atmosphere

155

was ripe for revival, and people were coming to the Lord. It was one last call.

I believe that's where we are now.[5]

Wanted: Empowered Disciples

There have been many great revivals and awakenings over the years, but few of these saw penitent new followers of Christ turn into the kind of disciples who would change the world.

Most theologians, scholars, pastors and faith leaders point to the first-century Church as our model since those believers did turn the world upside-down for Jesus Christ. How did they do that? Let's turn to the New Testament for the answer.

The Acts of the Apostles is often called the Acts of the Holy Spirit, who was acting through the apostles and followers of Christ in the earliest years of the Church. Before the ascension, Jesus gave them an important directive for their mission:

> "Do not leave Jerusalem, but wait for the gift my Father promised, which you have heard me speak about. For John baptized with water, but in a few days you will be baptized with the Holy Spirit."
>
> Acts 1:4–5

We will do nothing significant for the Kingdom of God without this infusion of power from the Holy Spirit. Yes, there are those who say that Spirit baptism is not for our age; that time is past. This lie has been propagated throughout the years by Satan himself so the Church of Jesus Christ would be powerless. As we read through the book of Acts, however, we find the Holy Spirit being poured out on believers repeatedly to empower them to do His work. The reason the Church has not been able to repeat the feats of the first century is lack of spiritual power.

Here are just two passages by way of illustration. First, Peter was preaching to the household of the Gentile Cornelius in Caesarea:

> While Peter was still speaking these words, the Holy Spirit came on all who heard the message. The circumcised believers who had come with Peter were astonished that the gift of the Holy Spirit had been poured out even on Gentiles. For they heard them speaking in tongues and praising God.
>
> Then Peter said, "Surely no one can stand in the way of their being baptized with water. They have received the Holy Spirit just as we have." So he ordered that they be baptized in the name of Jesus Christ.
>
> Acts 10:44–48

Then Paul was meeting up with new believers at Ephesus:

> There he found some disciples and asked them, "Did you receive the Holy Spirit when you believed?"
>
> They answered, "No, we have not even heard that there is a Holy Spirit."
>
> So Paul asked, "Then what baptism did you receive?"
>
> "John's baptism," they replied.
>
> Paul said, "John's baptism was a baptism of repentance. He told the people to believe in the one coming after him, that is, in Jesus." On hearing this, they were baptized in the name of the Lord Jesus. When Paul placed his hands on them, the Holy Spirit came on them, and they spoke in tongues and prophesied. There were about twelve men in all.
>
> Acts 19:1–7

In our time, labels seem to be important. For example, we label those Christians as charismatics or Pentecostals who experience and teach the baptism with the Holy Spirit—the supernatural experience of being filled with the Spirit's power. Yet first-century believers like Peter and Paul were not "charismatics" or "Pentecostals"—they were just empowered by the Holy Spirit, spoke in tongues and used various gifts of the Spirit.

A sincere but powerless Christian might exclaim, "I don't believe in the power of the Holy Spirit. That's for those Pentecostals!" We contend that denominational labels are divisive and not useful. In fact, they can be detrimental to our spiritual growth. It is time for us to cross denominational barriers and get back to the joy of simply following Jesus in all His power, glory and might.

The Gifts of the Spirit

Now about the gifts of the Spirit, brothers and sisters, I do not want you to be uninformed. You know that when you were pagans, somehow or other you were influenced and led astray to mute idols. Therefore I want you to know that no one who is speaking by the Spirit of God says, "Jesus be cursed," and no one can say, "Jesus is Lord," except by the Holy Spirit.

1 Corinthians 12:1–3

The apostle Paul is about to describe the gifts of the Holy Spirit operating in the Church in the first century. He does not want us to be uninformed or ignorant of these gifts. The same gifts are available today for those who earnestly desire them. But when was the last time you witnessed the gifts in operation in your church? Why is that?

We hear many explanations as to why the gifts are not at work in many sectors of the Church. None of these explanations hold up under scrutiny.

One of the main reasons for neglecting or rejecting the gifts is that they don't "look good" to nonbelievers and outsiders.

They can also be messy and hard to control. Churches love order and become uncomfortable when that order is upended. Most churches want to fit in with their communities and culture, and churches that practice the gifts of the Holy Spirit can be considered excessive or abnormal or worse. And then there is the theological position that dismisses the gifts as for the first-century Church only and not for today. The gifts, some say, are no longer needed.

Yet the gifts of the Holy Spirit are still in evidence today, especially in charismatic and Pentecostal churches.

Let's take a look at Paul's description of the operation of the gifts of the Spirit:

> There are different kinds of gifts, but the same Spirit distributes them. There are different kinds of service, but the same Lord. There are different kinds of working, but in all of them and in everyone it is the same God at work.
>
> Now to each one the manifestation of the Spirit is given for the common good. To one there is given through the Spirit a message of wisdom, to another a message of knowledge by means of the same Spirit, to another faith by the same Spirit, to another gifts of healing by that one Spirit, to another miraculous powers, to another prophecy, to another distinguishing between spirits, to another speaking in different kinds of tongues, and to still another the interpretation of tongues. All these are the work of one and the same Spirit, and he distributes them to each one, just as he determines.
>
> 1 Corinthians 12:4–11

If you want to grow in faith and in your assignment, seek to be filled with the Holy Spirit and empowered by Him with various gifts. Ask God intently and continuously for them to operate in your life. Walk in faith and pray for those who need physical healing or deliverance from oppression, drugs, alcohol, sex addictions or more. Find a body of believers who believe and walk in the gifts of the Spirit.

What gifts does God want you to have? We will talk more about that in chapter 14.

Mary Ann Peluso McGahan believes that time is short and that the Holy Spirit is moving and bringing in the harvest:

> We don't know how much time we have left, and we need boldness. So because of the urgency of the hour, the Holy Spirit is saying, "Get out there. Be bold. Don't be obnoxious but be bold."
>
> God is not interested in "seeker-sensitive." He is interested in Kingdom-sensitive. I hear a calling of the Spirit, as Noah did. It's time to get people into the Ark before the storm hits, before the Antichrist is revealed and before the end of all things.[6]

The key to being used by God in transformative ways—as Charles Finney, leader of the Second Great Awakening, wrote in *Power from on High,* and Puritan minister William Gurnall revealed in *The Christian in Complete Armor*—is using the gifts and power of the Holy Spirit. Peluso McGahan continues:

> The burden of the Lord on my heart is that as we see the harvest come in, we facilitate the baptism in the Holy Spirit for new converts. They need to be empowered before they go out into the world. The baptism in the Spirit gives you the power to live out your faith. We can have a Lamborghini or Maserati or Ferrari sitting right there, but if we don't have gas, that machine is not going anywhere.
>
> So I have a heart to see people baptized in the Holy Spirit, and for a strong prayer life, speaking and praying in the Spirit. And we need the power gifts—prophecy, healing and everything that 1 Corinthians 12 talks about. We need the power of the Holy Spirit.[7]

The Baptism with the Holy Spirit

It is important for us to understand just what the baptism in the Holy Spirit is, how we experience it, and, most importantly, how we use it in light of everything happening on planet earth. The best way to approach these questions is by reading the book of Acts, which describes the disciples being filled with the Holy Spirit.

Some argue that we are filled with the Spirit when we are saved. There is no question that, when we receive Christ as Savior, the Holy Spirit does the work and then indwells us. In Ephesians 1:13, for example, Paul says that "you also were included in Christ when you heard the message of truth, the gospel of your salvation. When you believed, you were marked in him with a seal, the promised Holy Spirit." But then why did Jesus tell His disciples, those who had believed and followed Him for three years, not to "leave Jerusalem, but wait for the gift my Father promised" (Acts 1:4) after He ascended? The Twelve, along with many other disciples, were filled with the Holy Spirit on the Day of Pentecost, as we saw in chapter 8.

And we noted in chapter 8 that, throughout the book of Acts, the Holy Spirit was poured out on believers repeatedly (for example, on the Samaritan believers in Acts 8:14–17) to empower them to do His work.

So we, too, must seek to be baptized in the Holy Spirit by praying earnestly and intensely for God to fill us to overflowing, and then wait on Him to do it supernaturally in us and through us.

I was born again in January 1974 while a senior in high school. Then I prayed earnestly and waited on God until, in April 1974, the Holy Spirit fell on many of us at the altar during a Sunday night service at church. I was filled with the Spirit with the evidence of speaking in tongues. (The months following

161

salvation were just my experience; many receive the baptism with the Spirit the same day they are saved, or soon after.)

I was a changed man. The Holy Spirit empowered me to do the work of the ministry. It was not a one-time experience; I continued over many years to seek the continued power and presence of the Holy Spirit; and I sought the spiritual gifts detailed in 1 Corinthians 12 (which we will discuss in chapter 14).

Often we stop at salvation and water baptism and do not follow through to receiving of the Holy Spirit. Transformation occurs, however, through the supernatural infilling and work of the Spirit.

One final note. The apostle Paul said that love is "the most excellent way" (1 Corinthians 12:31). Love must indeed be our primary goal. But Paul also said, "Follow the way of love and eagerly desire gifts of the Spirit, especially prophecy" (1 Corinthians 14:1). And remember what Jesus said: "Wait for the gift my Father promised" (Acts 1:4).

STRATEGIC SPIRITUAL EXERCISES

1. Take a good, hard look at your life. Are there ways your spiritual life has become stagnant?

2. If you have not been baptized in the Holy Spirit, begin asking the Father to fill you to overflowing every day. Do not stop asking for the rest of your life!

3. Read 1 Corinthians 12 every day for the next thirty days and ask God to give you the gifts He wants to use in your life.

4. Sign up for Spirit-filled conferences, classes and seminars.

5. Study the book of Acts and begin today or tomorrow to implement some of the principles and practices in your own life.

12

A TRUE FOLLOWER OF CHRIST

Let us think often that our only business in this life is to please
God. Perhaps all besides is but folly and vanity.

Brother Lawrence, *The Practice of the Presence of God*

Winter 1995. The Combined Maneuver Training Center (CMTC), Hohenfels, Germany.
We were lying prone on the ground near the top of a rolling
hill. Behind and below us were our medical and support troops,
setting up base camp for our rotation in the realistic training
area called "the box." We were up against the OPFOR (oppos-
ing force), a seasoned U.S. armor unit stationed year-round in
CMTC to train U.S. forces. They were hard to beat because
they knew the territory like the back of their hands.

"Sergeant," I said, "hand me those binoculars. I think I see
something coming up the road."

"Yes, sir," replied my chaplain assistant.

I lifted those powerful Army binoculars up to my eyes—only
to see something that brought the hairs on the back of my neck
straight up. It was a whole line of OPFOR armored vehicles

coming up the road right at us. They knew where we were but were still far enough out for us to react. We had only moments to warn the commander and others to evacuate the area.

I waved my arms above my head, yelling, "Let's roll, boys, OPFOR coming," as my sergeant and I ran down the hill to my vehicle. The other soldiers dropped everything, jumped into their vehicles and followed me out of the area. We got out just in the nick of time.

"Follow Me!"

The "Follow Me" statue—or, as some call it wrongly, "Iron Mike"—stands proudly in front of the Maneuver Center of Excellence headquarters at Fort Moore (formerly Fort Benning), Georgia. Many look on in awe, wondering how that statue received its name. It has an interesting history, as described in the *New York Times*:

> Aubrey S. Newman, the infantry colonel whose World War II battle cry of "Follow me!" became a watchword for infantry leadership and bravery, shouted the words while commanding a regiment leading Gen. Douglas MacArthur's "return" to the Philippines on Oct. 20, 1944—an amphibious assault on Leyte Island. As the beach landing stalled, his men became pinned down by Japanese fire. To save them, he rose and gave his now-famous command. The men then swept forward against the Japanese defenders. The cry became the motto of the 24th Infantry Division, and the Army depicted the incident on a recruiting poster that read: "Get up and get moving! Follow me!"[1]

Soldiers learn by watching others do the right things. We all learn by following great leaders, professors or mentors. But the ultimate learning comes from following our Head, Jesus Christ.

Jesus never said following Him would be easy or pain-free, but His Word promises that we receive eternal life when we give our lives to Him. But the rich young ruler turned down the offer to follow Jesus because the cost was too great. We will look at his story in just a moment.

A well-known principle that may have originated with Aristotle says, "He who cannot be a good follower cannot be a good leader." In the U.S. Army I learned that to be a good leader, you need to be a good follower. Remember what Jesus said to Peter:

> "Very truly I tell you, when you were younger you dressed yourself and went where you wanted; but when you are old you will stretch out your hands, and someone else will dress you and lead you where you do not want to go." Jesus said this to indicate the kind of death by which Peter would glorify God. Then he said to him, "Follow me!"
>
> John 21:18–19

The apostle Paul told the Philippian church: "Join together in following my example, brothers and sisters, and just as you have us as a model, keep your eyes on those who live as we do" (Philippians 3:17). In the same way, younger believers today should find a trusted spiritual mentor or group of believers who are mature in the Lord and who model mature Christian living.

What does it require to be a follower of Christ? Everything!

The Search for Happiness

Let's look at the story of the rich young ruler who turned down the offer to follow Jesus, and see how his story applies to our lives and the lives of those around us as followers of Jesus.

The story is found in three of the gospels: Matthew 19:16–30, Mark 10:17–31 and Luke 18:18–30. In studying these passages, we can deduce several important things about this man who is asking Jesus about eternal life. He is a man of authority, power and position, as is suggested by his title—in the Greek, *archon*: "a ruler, governor, leader, leading man; with the Jews, an official member (a member of the executive) of the assembly of elders."[2]

Possibly he was the ruler of the local synagogue and a Pharisee, because of his interest in the Torah and the commandments. He was probably a Jew since no Roman officer or official would query Jesus about a religious matter; most likely a Jew would be concerned about the Law or Torah. We know that he was not only rich, but in the elite class of rich or super-rich ("extremely" wealthy—in the Greek, *sphodra*). But although he had great wealth ("many possessions"), he could not figure out how to guarantee his entrance into the Kingdom of God. And finally he was young (*neaniskos* in Greek, Matthew 19:22), a span between his early twenties to forty.

Let's read the story in Luke 18:18–27:

> A certain ruler asked [Jesus], "Good teacher, what must I do to inherit eternal life?"
>
> "Why do you call me good?" Jesus answered. "No one is good—except God alone. You know the commandments: 'You shall not commit adultery, you shall not murder, you shall not steal, you shall not give false testimony, honor your father and mother.'"
>
> "All these I have kept since I was a boy," he said.
>
> When Jesus heard this, he said to him, "You still lack one thing. Sell everything you have and give to the poor, and you will have treasure in heaven. Then come, follow me."
>
> When he heard this, he became very sad, because he was very wealthy. Jesus looked at him and said, "How hard it is for the rich to enter the kingdom of God! Indeed, it is easier for a

camel to go through the eye of a needle than for someone who is rich to enter the kingdom of God."

Those who heard this asked, "Who then can be saved?"

Jesus replied, "What is impossible with man is possible with God."

We can learn some lessons about being a true follower of Christ from this man who possessed everything the world says is of utmost importance: wealth, status, power and youth. Yet he was not satisfied! He yearned for the one thing money cannot buy: eternal life. He thought He might find this in Jesus, but he was not willing to pay the price.

Most people today are searching for happiness. But clinical psychologist and author Jordan Peterson states:

> It's all very well to think the meaning of life is happiness, but what happens when you're unhappy? Happiness is a great side effect. When it comes, accept it gratefully. But it's fleeting and unpredictable. It's not something to aim at—because it's not an aim. And if happiness is the purpose of life, what happens when you're unhappy? Then you're a failure. And perhaps a suicidal failure. Happiness is like cotton candy. It's just not going to do the job.[3]

Actor and comedian Jim Carrey once said, "I think everybody should get rich and famous and do everything they ever dreamed of, so they can see that it's not the answer."[4]

But if riches, fame, prestige, power, youth and even happiness are not ultimately satisfying, then what is?

The answer has always been and will always be Jesus. We must learn at some point in our lives, like the rich young ruler, that nothing the world's system has to offer can truly satisfy the longing of the heart. Our hearts are made to have union with our Maker.

Here is one more lesson from the young man. When he approached Jesus, he called Him "good teacher," and the response from Jesus was eternal. (Isn't it always that way with Jesus?)

"Why do you call me good?" Jesus answered. "No one is good— except God alone."

Luke 18:19

Let's translate this exchange so it is understandable. The rich young ruler was using the phrase *good teacher* as a courtesy, even a pretense to get on Jesus' good side. But Jesus was telling the young man that he did not understand who Jesus is: the Lord of the universe. Jesus was telling him, "Do you know who you are talking to? I *am* God!"

To be a true follower of Christ, and thereby fulfill our purpose and mission, we must understand who God is. He is:

- The great I AM (Exodus 3:14)
- Wonderful Counselor, Mighty God, Everlasting Father, Prince of Peace (Isaiah 9:6)
- The Redeemer (Isaiah 59:20)
- Immanuel, God with us (Matthew 1:23)
- King of the Jews (Matthew 27:37)
- The Lamb of God (John 1:29)
- The bread of life (John 6:35)
- The living Stone (1 Peter 2:4)
- The First and the Last (Revelation 1:17)
- The Living One (Revelation 1:18)
- King of Kings and Lord of Lords (Revelation 19:16)
- The Alpha and the Omega (Revelation 22:13)

Whom Are You Following?

Soldiers will follow a proven and trusted leader. Just look at one heroic leader in the Normandy invasion, Brigadier General Norman "Dutch" Cota. Cota was made deputy commander of the 29th Infantry Division, and part of his job was to help the 29th Infantry Division overcome a fear of combat that had developed. War History Online recounts Cota's D-Day landing on Omaha Beach on June 6, 1944:

> As he had predicted, the situation he landed in was confused, a tangled mess of men and equipment. . . . As the troops started pushing off the beach, Cota strode up and down the slope, personally urging men on through minefields and past litters of dead bodies.
>
> When a group of Rangers became pinned down near Vierville, Cota led by example. He walked out across the open ground ahead of them. When he wasn't immediately gunned down, the Rangers followed him. . . .
>
> For his action on D-Day, Cota was awarded the Silver Star by the Americans and the Distinguished Service Order by the British.[5]

The troops of Brigadier General Cota were willing to follow him into harm's way because he led them from the front. He was not afraid to take the lead despite heavy gunfire from the Germans. He had been with the troops in training, and now he was with them in combat. He not only talked the talk but walked the walk.

Jesus also leads us by example. He came down from His glorious throne in heaven and became a man. He grew up among His people, performed miracles and healings, went willingly to the cross to suffer and die for us, rose from the dead three days later, and then, forty days later, ascended to heaven to sit at the right hand of God, the Father almighty. As our great Intercessor in heaven, He will be with us every step of the way. As the Bible tells us in Hebrews 4:14–16:

> Since we have a great high priest who has ascended into heaven, Jesus the Son of God, let us hold firmly to the faith we profess. For we do not have a high priest who is unable to empathize with our weaknesses, but we have one who has been tempted in every way, just as we are—yet he did not sin. Let us then approach God's throne of grace with confidence, so that we may receive mercy and find grace to help us in our time of need.

Just as Brigadier General Cota told his officers before D-Day, life can be difficult, complex, confusing. But on Omaha Beach he did not just give instructions to his troops; he led them by example. How much more can we trust Jesus, our Intercessor and great High Priest, to lead us in our lives? He knows better than we do what we need, how we should live, whom we should marry, where we need to go, and what mission He has called us to carry out.

Troy Miller, president of National Religious Broadcasters, an international association of Christian communicators, points out that becoming a follower of Christ takes intent. He explains:

> You have to be intentional about following Christ in today's world because so many things are thrown at us to distract us from our real purpose—not only from following Christ, but following Him in service and doing the work He has called us to do.
>
> Each of us has been uniquely and wonderfully made. Christ has given us gifts that help us proclaim the Gospel. He may have you in evangelism. Maybe He has you doing something in social services. Maybe He has you preaching or teaching Scripture.

Maybe you're working with kids. But whatever it is, you have to be intentional about it in today's world.

We also have to remember that Jesus said, "Lo, I am with you always." We may sometimes seem to be alone in the world, but Christ is always with us. That always brings me back to understand that I am *not* alone here. Christ has called me to do this, He has gifted me to do this, and He is equipping me every day to be able to serve and follow Him.[6]

Following Christ is a moment-by-moment exercise, just as Brother Lawrence, a lay brother who worked in the kitchen of a monastery in seventeenth-century Paris, said at the beginning of this chapter: "Our only business in this life is to please God."

It is important for us as followers of Jesus to keep our eyes on Him. Where is He leading me today? Whom will He place in my path? What act of service can I perform today? Whom can I tell about Jesus?

It is the little things we do every day that add up in the end to what we all want to hear when we enter the gates of heaven: "Well done, good and faithful servant" (Matthew 25:21).

══ STRATEGIC SPIRITUAL EXERCISES ══

1. Think of the mature believers in your life whom you trust. What can you learn from their example? What principles can you apply to your life?

2. Meditate on Jesus' words to Peter in John 21:18–19. What does it mean for you to follow Jesus? Write down three things you can do today to follow Him more closely.

3. Read Hebrews 4:14–16 every day for the next week. How does understanding the ministry of Jesus, your

great High Priest, intensify your determination to follow Him?

4. Start practicing a few minutes every day when you just sit and listen, without distraction, to the Holy Spirit's whispering to your heart. What is He saying?

13

THE COMMANDER
OF THE HEAVENLY HOST

And it came to pass, when Joshua was by Jericho, that he lifted
his eyes and looked, and behold, a Man stood opposite him with
His sword drawn in His hand. And Joshua went to Him and said
to Him, "Are You for us or for our adversaries?" So He said, "No,
but as Commander of the army of the LORD I have now come."

Joshua 5:13–14 NKJV

Late spring 1990. Dhahran Air Base, Eastern Province, Saudi Arabia. "Chaplain,
the brigade commander wants to see you right away," said my
executive officer.

I gulped. Anytime a senior commander wants to see you right
away, it cannot be good. An infantry brigade commander is a
fearsome thing, especially to a young captain chaplain. I had
been on active duty for less than a year. Colonels and above
scared me. And this one was a tough, no-nonsense infantry
officer with little time for small talk.

"Sir, you wanted to see me?" I asked as I poked my head
into his office.

"Chaplain, come on in. I have a mission for you," he exclaimed.

I walked in and took a seat in front of his desk.

"I want you to start sensitivity training with our troops right away concerning their sexual orientation."

It was one of those moments when time slowed down. I searched for a reply for this grizzled, combat-hardened infantry officer. I studied his face for any sign of a smirk or smile. Was he dead serious? I could not tell, but I was sweating bullets. My career could be on the line. But there was no way I was going to comply.

I blurted out my reply. "I'm sorry, sir. You can have my resignation and rank in the morning."

He broke out into a loud belly laugh.

"Chaplain, I just wanted to see what you were going to say. You just made my day. Now get out of here."

He had been joking with me. I breathed a sigh of relief and left his office.

Commanders in the military have great authority and great responsibility. They are ultimately responsible for everyone and everything in their units. There are different levels of command in the U.S. Army, all the way from captains over hundreds to four-star generals over hundreds of thousands. The entire U.S. military has only one commander-in-chief, however, and that is the President of the United States (POTUS). POTUS has the ultimate command authority.

It is interesting to note that the U.S. military is run by civilians and not military officers. The Secretary of the Army, the Secretary of Defense and POTUS are all civilians. It is the same for the Navy, Air Force and other branches of the U.S. military. The highest-ranking military officer in U.S. government is the four-star Chairman of the Joint Chiefs of Staff, who takes orders from the Secretary of Defense. The forefathers who wrote the Constitution did not want the military to try to overthrow the government in a coup.

Just as the entire military follows the orders of POTUS, so the Church of Jesus Christ follows the orders of her Commander-in-Chief, our Lord Jesus Christ. He directs all assignments and instills His purpose in each of His followers. We all march to the beat of His resounding drums.

Commander and Conquering Warrior

The Commander of the heavenly host is coming back to earth to subdue the final rebellion against Him. It is exciting to see the picture from Revelation:

> Now I saw heaven opened, and behold, a white horse. And He who sat on him was called Faithful and True, and in righteousness He judges and makes war. His eyes were like a flame of fire, and on His head were many crowns. He had a name written that no one knew except Himself. He was clothed with a robe dipped in blood, and His name is called The Word of God. And the armies in heaven, clothed in fine linen, white and clean, followed Him on white horses. Now out of His mouth goes a sharp sword, that with it He should strike the nations. And He Himself will rule them with a rod of iron. He Himself treads the winepress of the fierceness and wrath of Almighty God. And He has on His robe and on His thigh a name written: KING OF KINGS AND LORD OF LORDS.
>
> Revelation 19:11–16 NKJV

Ever since the fall of Satan, and then of Adam and Eve in the Garden, humanity has been at war. But when Jesus Christ, our Lord and Savior, returns to the earth, it will be as conquering Warrior. The armies clothed in white and riding on white horses behind Him is the Church triumphant, which is us!

Don't worry, if you have never been in the Army or ridden a horse, you will be in your glorified body and well able to perform all the tasks the Commander asks. We can have the utmost trust and confidence in Jesus' leadership, authority and power!

Retired U.S. Army Chaplain (Colonel) Peter Brzezinski reflects on all the battle imagery in the Bible:

> I think the Lord uses military language frequently in Scripture, in both Old and New Testaments, to help us understand the reality that there is a spiritual battle going on. We don't always recognize it, and we are frequently numb to it, because it's not that plain to see. But it's real. When you love the Lord and are in step with the Spirit and seek to serve, you do sense the battle. In fact, many times, when there's resistance, when things are not going smoothly, that's an authentication that you're in the right place.
>
> So I believe the Lord has put battle imagery in Scripture for us to understand the struggle between good and evil, and that our main archenemy is the devil and his wicked angels and minions who seek to destroy God's people or distract us from His plan and purpose that He put us here for.[1]

Retired Lieutenant General William G. "Jerry" Boykin, the U.S. Deputy Undersecretary of Defense for Intelligence under President George W. Bush, agrees that the Bible is very clear that we are in a spiritual battle. General Boykin, who during his 36-year career in the military was part of Delta Force and involved in many high-profile missions, emphasizes that we need to be prepared:

> The moment we turn our lives over to Jesus Christ to make Him our Redeemer, we are in a spiritual battle, and we are up against a real enemy. As 1 Peter 5:8 says, our adversary, Satan, walks about like a roaring lion. Just stop and think about that.

We need to go to Ephesians 6 and understand the whole concept of spiritual warfare. There are two themes that run through Ephesians 6: praying and reading God's Word. So what do we need to do? We need to pray and read the Word.

If you're not reading and absorbing God's Word every day, you're not going to be battle-ready.[2]

Paul McGuire, an internationally recognized prophecy expert, believes that America is experiencing the greatest battle for hearts and minds in its history. McGuire, a commentator on CNN, Fox News and the History Channel, co-author of the bestseller *The Babylon Code* and many other books, and former host of the nationally syndicated *Paul McGuire Show*, explains:

America is a soft target for the forces of the Antichrist. We're in a struggle for freedom in America, and we have taken our freedoms and liberties for granted. I know many mighty people of God, but the majority of those who call themselves Christians, sad to say, are not in the spiritual battle. Yet the Lord through His Spirit is calling individuals—and they know who they are—to enlist in His spiritual army for the last days.[3]

Before Jesus ascended into heaven, He told His followers to wait for "power from on high" (Luke 24:49 NKJV). McGuire says:

The actual translation of that phrase *power from on high* comes from the Greek word *dunamis*, which means the explosive, dynamite power of God.

When we think of the Church, we don't think of earthly militancy or earthly violence. We think of the love of God and setting people free. But if you're going to set people free, you have to knock out the enemy of man's souls, which is the devil and the levels of demonic power trying to control America and the rest of the world. And the only way you can knock out that demonic power is to use the precise weaponry and training Jesus gave us when He told us that we need to be clothed with "power from on high"—*dunamis*, the dynamite, explosive power of God.[4]

As the apostle Paul wrote in Ephesians 6:12 (NKJV), "We do not wrestle against flesh and blood, but against principalities, against powers, against the rulers of the darkness of this age, against spiritual hosts of wickedness in the heavenly places." So, McGuire continues,

We have to raise the level of our game. The Church is called to occupy until Jesus comes (Luke 19:13). This is not a military occupation. It's an occupation of servanthood and love, because servanthood and love equate with the greatest power on heaven and earth, and we must be an extension of the power and love of the Kingdom of God until Jesus returns.

God is talking about our learning to walk in the power of the Holy Spirit, and using and accessing the mind of Christ—bringing in from the invisible realm into our physical reality biblically authentic power, motivation and a sound mind, for God has not given us a spirit of fear. When you have a sound mind, your mind is operating in that razor-sharp dynamic that consists of a double-edged sword—part of the full armor of God.

And let me just push the envelope further. I believe that the full armor of God, if we could see it in the invisible realm, is really an exoskeleton. It could have been designed by DARPA [Defense Advanced Research Projects Agency] or one of the scientific military branches, because it is armor that goes beyond metal, swords, leather shoes and your traditional or conventional armor during the Roman Empire. The armor we wear as modern Christians would make Elon Musk weep for jealousy as he watched us, the Body of Christ, turn on all the various "apps" God has given us and downloaded into us by faith.

How to Overcome the Enemy

We saw in the Scripture at the very beginning of this chapter that Joshua, warrior and successor to Moses, encountered "a man . . . with a drawn sword in his hand" (Joshua 5:13).

Who was this man? He could have been an archangel, but more likely He was the preincarnate Lord Jesus Christ Himself. How do we know this? Because He was "commander of the army of the LORD" (verse 14). Because Joshua "fell facedown to the ground in reverence, and asked Him, 'What message does my Lord have for his servant?'" (verse 14). And because we read in the very next chapter, "The LORD said to Joshua" (6:2), probably part of the same encounter.

It is interesting to note that the Lord was not siding with Joshua, but challenging Joshua to side with Him: "As commander of the army of the LORD I have now come" (Joshua 5:14). And the Man told Joshua the Lord had come to instruct Joshua in detail how the Israelites were to overcome the enemies of God:

> Then the LORD said to Joshua, "See, I have delivered Jericho into your hands, along with its king and its fighting men. March around the city once with all the armed men. Do this for six days. Have seven priests carry trumpets of rams' horns in front of the ark. On the seventh day, march around the city seven times, with the priests blowing the trumpets. When you hear them sound a long blast on the trumpets, have the whole army give a loud shout; then the wall of the city will collapse and the army will go up, everyone straight in."
>
> Joshua 6:2–5

This is a template on how God instructs us. You may ask, "Why doesn't God speak to me in such direct terms?" One answer is that God does speak to us all the time, but we are distracted by so many things that the message gets overlooked or garbled. We need to get alone and quiet before the Commander to hear His voice. It takes training, time, patience and a willingness to lay aside all the distractions that life throws our way.

The Lord knows the end from the beginning. He exists over time and space. There is no obstacle so great that it can thwart His plans. He knows exactly how to defeat the enemy and gain victory—not only for Joshua and the Israelites, but for you as well. You do not always understand everything God is doing in your life, but live by faith in Him who knows no limits, and listen for His voice.

We tell people all the time who have incredibly difficult circumstances that although we may not have the answer to their dilemma, we know the One who does have the answer. He may not choose to disclose it right now, but rest assured of His faithfulness. Also, total answers may not come this side of eternity.

You may read the above passage and exclaim that it made no sense to march around the most heavily fortified city of that era and expect the walls to fall down. According to archaeologists:

The mound, or "tell," of Jericho was surrounded by a great earthen rampart, or embankment, with a stone retaining wall at its base. The retaining wall was some 12–15 ft high. On top of that was a mudbrick wall 6 ft thick and about 20–26 ft high. . . . At the crest of the embankment was a similar mudbrick wall whose base was roughly 46 ft above the ground level outside the retaining wall. This is what loomed high above the Israelites as they marched around the city each day for seven days. Humanly speaking, it was impossible for the Israelites to penetrate the impregnable bastion of Jericho.[5]

God's orders and directions to us do not always make sense. It is not our job to tell Him what to do or understand all the why's of His guidance. The life of faith is not a democracy. It is a theocracy—"the rule of God"—in which we follow the orders of the One who is in charge. God does not need our counsel or vote. Paul wrote, "Who has known the mind of the Lord? Or who has been his counselor?" (Romans 11:34).

The real question is: Do I trust my Commander? If the answer is yes, then we must follow His lead. If it is no, then we cannot say we are followers of Christ. Many who claim to be Christians do not trust the Lord to guide them. You cannot claim to be a Christian and not do what the Master asks of you. He said:

> "If you want to be my disciple, you must, by comparison, hate everyone else—your father and mother, wife and children, brothers and sisters—yes, even your own life. Otherwise, you cannot be my disciple. And if you do not carry your own cross and follow me, you cannot be my disciple."
>
> Luke 14:26–27 NLT

Jesus is not saying that you must hate your loved ones. He is saying that you cannot place your love and allegiance to others above your relationship with Him. He comes first in all your relationships and priorities.

You have probably heard people say they do not want to ask the Lord to lead them for fear that He might send them to Africa or some other place they do not wish to go. But this is almost laughable. To be a follower, you must be willing to follow! Listen to the apostle Paul's counsel to Timothy: "Join with me in suffering, like a good soldier of Christ Jesus. No one serving as a soldier gets entangled in civilian affairs, but rather tries to please his commanding officer" (2 Timothy 2:3–4). Carrying your cross means denying your own desires, wants and needs in order to please Him. Besides, Jesus knows your needs far better than you do.

Colonel Brzezinski expands on Paul's image of being "a good soldier of Jesus Christ":

> It's much like physical training in the military. You go through it, train up and go through tests. Then you kind of ramp down. Then you maintain it. And then you go through it again. I think those cyclic things go on in our spiritual lives as well. God allows trials and tribulations to strengthen us and develop those muscles. What keeps us going and even gives us joy in those times is knowing the end—that Jesus wins and that we're on the winning team.
>
> We don't always see it that way. We see suffering as "I must be doing something wrong." But when it's for the sake of the Gospel—when you're in a spiritual battle and standing up for the Lord as a servant and soldier for Him, and you get shot at— Paul says that's a blessing. This perspective helps us take a pause and, as we say in the military, exercise "battlefield patience." Wait for a moment and see what it's about before you respond or react. That goes a long way to help us, whatever stage we're in, when we go through challenges in life.[6]

Learning to Trust

Joshua did not learn to trust God overnight. In fact, he learned not only his leadership skills but his trust in God by following Moses for forty years in the desert.

Remember that, near the very beginning of those forty years, Joshua and Caleb were the only two of twelve spies who gave a good report of the Promised Land when returning to Moses. The twelve had been sent to explore the land and report on what they found. Ten of them said that although the land had great promise and wonderful produce, it was also filled with large, fortified cities and giants (Nephilim) who would defeat them.

So, although God had promised the Israelites that land, the people gave in to fear and rebelled against Moses and Aaron. We read what happened in Numbers 14:4–10:

> They said to each other, "We should choose a leader and go back to Egypt."
>
> Then Moses and Aaron fell facedown in front of the whole Israelite assembly gathered there. Joshua son of Nun and Caleb son of Jephunneh, who were among those who had explored the land, tore their clothes and said to the entire Israelite assembly, "The land we passed through and explored is exceedingly good. If the LORD is pleased with us, he will lead us into that land, a land flowing with milk and honey, and will give it to us. Only do not rebel against the LORD. And do not be afraid of the people of the land, because we will devour them. Their protection is gone, but the LORD is with us. Do not be afraid of them."
>
> But the whole assembly talked about stoning them.

We must be very careful not to complain about our assignment or rebel against God's authority. As He delivered the Israelites from Egypt, He would also lead them into conquering the Promised Land—but He required that they trust Him.

Joshua and Caleb were the only spies who believed God's promises. The other ten, plus the entire assembly of Israel aged twenty or older, after rebelling, did not live to see the Promised Land. They camped in the desert for forty years until they all died.

Joshua learned many valuable lessons on the journey to and into the Promised Land, most of all to trust in his Commander-in-Chief.

We can learn a lot from the wilderness experiences of life. They have a way of shaping us so we lean more and more on our heavenly Father. And when we follow the Lord faithfully, we mature in our relationship with Him, grow in the grace of God and understand what it is to be a true follower of Christ, no matter the circumstances.

STRATEGIC SPIRITUAL EXERCISES

1. Think about a time in your life when you followed the Lord despite difficult circumstances. How did it make you feel? Did you grow from it? What did you learn?

2. Reread the appearance of Jesus, the Commander of the armies, in Revelation 19:11–16. Is He different from the Jesus we read about in the Gospels? What is it about Jesus the Commander that inspires you?

3. What does Luke 14:26–27 say to you personally about picking up your cross and following Jesus?

4. Review the report of Joshua and Caleb in Numbers 14:1–9. What do you learn from their courage and faith? How can you apply these to your own life?

PART 4

USING YOUR GIFTS

14

YOUR ASSIGNMENT AND YOUR GIFTS

So whether you eat or drink or whatever you do, do it all for the glory of God.

1 Corinthians 10:31

Summer 2008. Presidential Tower, Crystal City, Virginia. I could not believe what I was seeing on the overhead screens at our semiannual U.S. Army chaplains' personnel assignments conference.

I was one of twelve chaplain assignment managers. We were there making individual assignments on behalf of the Army chief of chaplains, who has overall responsibility for ensuring that the right chaplain is assigned to the right command. We were sitting around an oval table, representing different commands throughout the Army, and we had assignments to make for more than five hundred officers. Each assignment required that we look over thirty attributes for each officer. The screens, one officer at a time, showed each officer's record, photo, all previous assignments, rank, combat time, education, abilities, preferences and a host of other attributes. And we had to hammer out each and every assignment in just one week. A daunting task, for sure!

I was proud of the way we searched for just the right officer to fill the important assignment the Army had for him or her. But I wondered during that difficult process how God forms us with gifts and abilities and then sends us out into the world to make a difference for His Kingdom. A daunting task for us, but not for the Almighty! He searches our hearts and minds, and endows each of us with passions, gifts and abilities. No two people are alike. Even identical twins have their own unique personality and function.

This chapter is designed to help you find the passions, gifts and abilities God has placed in you.

Taking Inventory

It is vitally important for you to stop and take inventory of who you are in Christ, the gifts and talents He has given you and how you can use them in your life.

Your life is a gift from God and He expects you to use your gifts to the best of your ability. You do not want to be like the man in Jesus' story whose master gave him a talent and he went out and buried it. Jesus said:

"He also who had received the one talent came forward, saying, 'Master, I knew you to be a hard man, reaping where you did not sow, and gathering where you scattered no seed, so I was afraid, and I went and hid your talent in the ground. Here, you have what is yours.' But his master answered him, 'You wicked and slothful servant! You knew that I reap where I have not sown and gather where I scattered no seed? Then you ought to have invested my money with the bankers, and at my coming I should have received what was my own with interest.

"'So take the talent from him and give it to him who has the ten talents. For to everyone who has will more be given, and he will have an abundance. But from the one who has not, even what he has will be taken away. And cast the worthless servant into the outer darkness. In that place there will be weeping and gnashing of teeth.'"

Matthew 25:24–30 ESV

This is not about works; it is about faithfulness and obedience to Christ and His call on our lives. The Lord has called each of us not only to follow Him, but to rightly use the gifts He has given us to serve His Kingdom. There are those who fear using the magnificent gifts given to them by the Lord of the universe. But by stepping out in faith and using their gifts in accordance with God's design for their lives, they will discover the incredible destiny their Creator planned for them "before the foundation of the world" (Ephesians 1:4 NKJV).

Natural Gifts

Natural gifts are the God-given abilities, strengths, talents, passions and skills that God has placed in your DNA and that are passed down through your lineage.

Sometimes extraordinary gifts are present in the very young, who are called child prodigies. Wolfgang Amadeus Mozart, for example, was composing little pieces at age five, traveled Europe as a keyboard performer from age six, composed his first symphony at eight and his first opera at twelve. While his musical genius was obvious early on, his father, also a gifted musician, played an important role in developing young Mozart's talents. Did Mozart inherit these gifts through his parents' DNA? Unquestionably yes.

History abounds with geniuses such as Plato, Aristotle, Leonardo da Vinci, Michelangelo, Einstein and countless more. But God has given everyone on planet earth gifts and abilities, many of whom never develop or even discover them, for many reasons, including poverty, poor health, lack of opportunity and lack of mentorship.

Ephesians 1:11–12 (MSG) offers an encouraging message regarding the gifts and talents God has given each of us:

> It's in Christ that we find out who we are and what we are living for. Long before we first heard of Christ and got our hopes up, he had his eye on us, had designs on us for glorious living, part of the overall purpose he is working out in everything and everyone.

The question remains: How do I discover those gifts, talents, abilities and passions that God has put within me? First and foremost, if you are a follower of Christ, ask our heavenly Father, as Jesus taught:

> "Ask and it will be given to you; seek and you will find; knock and the door will be opened to you. For everyone who asks receives; the one who seeks finds; and to the one who knocks, the door will be opened.
>
> "Which of you, if your son asks for bread, will give him a stone? Or if he asks for a fish, will give him a snake? If you, then, though you are evil, know how to give good gifts to your children, how much more will your Father in heaven give good gifts to those who ask him!"
>
> Matthew 7:7–11

Asking may seem superficial, but prayer is the most potent force in the universe. If you ask God to reveal to you the gifts He has given you, He will! The answer may come in any number of ways—maybe through a teacher who sees that gift in you, a parent or mentor who encourages you, a passion in which you excel, or in another completely unexpected way. The truth is, God will answer. Watch for it.

I mentioned in chapter 2 that I have a passion for the saxophone. In my journey, it happened in an unexpected way. I was about six or seven, sitting with my dad on the living room couch watching *The Ed Sullivan Show*, a popular television variety program. One of the performers that night was a saxophone player named Boots Randolph, playing with his band. Suddenly I exclaimed, "Dad, I want to play the sax!"

My passion for the sax was so great that I spent up to eight hours a day practicing. After graduating with a B.A. in music and a concentration in saxophone performance, and then all during my career in the U.S. Army, I continued with the sax. I have played it literally all over the world in every kind of music venue and genre you can imagine—gospel, blues, rock, pop, classical, jazz, country, Dixieland . . . the list is endless.

You never know when and where you will discover your gifts, but be aware that those gifts inside you are waiting to spring forth. As the apostle Paul wrote to the Romans:

> I say, through the grace given to me, to everyone who is among you, not to think of himself more highly than he ought to think, but to think soberly, as God has dealt to each one a measure of faith. For as we have many members in one body, but all the members do not have the same function, so we, being many, are one body in Christ, and individually members of one another. Having then gifts differing according to the grace that is given to us, let us use them: if prophecy, let us prophesy in proportion to our faith; or ministry, let us use it in our ministering; he who teaches, in teaching; he who exhorts, in exhortation; he who gives, with liberality; he who leads, with diligence; he who shows mercy, with cheerfulness.
>
> Romans 12:3–8 NKJV

About these natural gifts, retired U.S. Army Chaplain (Colonel) Scott McChrystal says:

> The amazing thing about the army of God is that we each have roles, responsibilities, missions. We are truly contributing members. God says in His Word that every person has been given "a measure of faith" and that every person has been given some kind of gifting. What a transformation it is to see somebody find and employ that gift in accomplishing a mission![1]

Some people use scientific methodologies like personality tests and performance-based metrics to discover their strengths. And these do have a measure of success. But most do not give you a complete picture of your true self, simply because we are very complex beings.

If you say you have no gifts, or at least that you have not discovered them yet, our response is always the same: "What do others say about your abilities?" You are not always the best judge of your abilities, and you may not understand your own strengths and weaknesses.

Supernatural Gifts

Just as there are natural gifts springing up from our DNA, so also there are supernatural gifts springing up from the Holy Spirit within us. (We talked about these in chapter 11.) The apostle Paul writes:

> There are different kinds of gifts, but the same Spirit distributes them. There are different kinds of service, but the same Lord. There are different kinds of working, but in all of them and in everyone it is the same God at work.

> 1 Corinthians 12:4–6

Paul goes on to teach about these gifts:

> Now to each one the manifestation of the Spirit is given for the common good. To one there is given through the Spirit a message of wisdom, to another a message of knowledge by means of the same Spirit, to another faith by the same Spirit, to another gifts of healing by that one Spirit, to another miraculous powers, to another prophecy, to another distinguishing between spirits, to another speaking in different kinds of tongues, and to still another the interpretation of tongues. All these are the work of one and the same Spirit, and he distributes them to each one, just as he determines.
>
> verses 7–11

The manifestation and demonstration of the supernatural gifts, Paul states, are "for the common good," with the express purpose of glorifying God and edifying or building up the Church, the followers of Jesus. Every time the Spirit of God uses you in one or more of the gifts, you and all around you are being edified.

You may ask, "How do I get these gifts and how do I operate in them?" Good question!

In my own journey, I have meditated on the listing of gifts in 1 Corinthians 12 to see which ones I would like to have and operate in. I have watched those I trusted minister in those gifts to see how God used them. I talked with some and asked their views on the use of the gifts. Over time I have asked God in prayer for those gifts. And at some point, when I sensed God leading me to operate in one of them, I stepped out in faith.

So far in my faith journey, I have been used by God in the gifts of healing, prophecy, faith, discernment of spirits, and speaking and interpreting tongues.

A word of wisdom and caution is needed here. Contrary to popular belief, stepping out to use a gift will not always go smoothly or perfectly. We are imperfect people. We will make mistakes and need correction. And experienced pastors always need to monitor the gifts being manifested and discern whether they are from God.

All the gifts operate by faith in God alone. So it is good to talk these principles over with trusted friends, leaders and pastors. If a person has never operated in the gifts of the Holy Spirit, talk with someone who has.

Yes, abuse of the gifts occurs. Emotions often run high, and the saints of God sometimes put on displays of the flesh to be seen for show by others. But don't let that stop you from exploring the gifts God wants you to have.

Retired U.S. Army Chaplain (Colonel) Peter Brzezinski says he is reminded of the passage in Ephesians:

> To each one of us grace has been given as Christ apportioned it. This is why it says: "When he ascended on high, he took many captives and gave gifts to his people." . . .
>
> Christ himself gave the apostles, the prophets, the evangelists, the pastors and teachers, to equip his people for works of service, so that the body of Christ may be built up until we all reach unity in the faith and in the knowledge of the Son of God and become mature, attaining to the whole measure of the fullness of Christ.
>
> Ephesians 4:7–8, 11–13

Brzezinski explains:

> This passage tells me that God is infinitely interested in our having the gifts and tools we need out of His love to do the work He calls us to do.
>
> He doesn't call you to do things you're not made to do. He calls you to do things you *are* made to do, and He knows what those things are. You must discover them as you go. Show Him

humility. And, in fact, Scripture says that "without faith it is impossible to please Him" (Hebrews 11:6 NKJV). So our walk is by faith. We walk by faith and not by sight—faith in God and His work and love for us.

As you get assignments along the way, He works in tandem with your gifts and desires and interests that He's woven into your life—not by accident, not by mistake. Now you have to trust and take the next right step. Sometimes we can't see the whole picture; we just know we're supposed to do something. And He leads us to that thing.[2]

Colonel Brzezinski draws from his experience in the U.S. Army:

I thought I was going from A to B because of something I needed to do. Well, that was only part of the story. Because the biggest piece of all is this: When He moves you from A to B, and gives you those orders or assignments or gifts, it's always, always about His work, which is with the people you're going to interact with. You have something they need, and they have something you need, and together you continue to march forward and get the work done for the Lord.

I think that's how we use God's assignments and gifts to accomplish His work. We all have gifts. Scripture lays them out—teaching, preaching, evangelism, administration, helps, mercy, kindness and more. There's a long list of the gifts God has given His people, in several chapters—Romans 12, 1 Corinthians 12, Ephesians 4, 1 Peter 4 and other places. Other people can help you realize and see and develop your gifts to be an even more effective soldier for Him.[3]

A Final Word

The gifts of the Holy Spirit are for the Body of Christ. And the gifts are for today. Why else would Paul go to such great lengths to explain their use in the Body of Christ?

But nobody has all the gifts:

> You are the body of Christ, and each one of you is a part of it. And God has placed in the church first of all apostles, second prophets, third teachers, then miracles, then gifts of healing, of helping, of guidance, and of different kinds of tongues. Are all apostles? Are all prophets? Are all teachers? Do all work miracles? Do all have gifts of healing? Do all speak in tongues? Do all interpret? Now eagerly desire the greater gifts.
>
> 1 Corinthians 12:27–31

Paul also puts the gifts into perspective, showing us "the most excellent way" (verse 31):

> If I speak in the tongues of men or of angels, but do not have love, I am only a resounding gong or a clanging cymbal. If I have the gift of prophecy and can fathom all mysteries and all knowledge, and if I have a faith that can move mountains, but do not have love, I am nothing. If I give all I possess to the poor and give over my body to hardship that I may boast, but do not have love, I gain nothing.
>
> 1 Corinthians 13:1–3

The love of God is the essential foundation of everything we do. The gifts of the Spirit should flow out of the love of God. It is vital that we earnestly seek and desire the supernatural gifts so we can use them effectively to build up the Church—and always in love.

STRATEGIC SPIRITUAL EXERCISES

1. List your strengths and weaknesses. What do they say about you and your direction in life?

2. What are your natural abilities, gifts and passions? Share these with someone who knows you and whom you trust. Are there any discrepancies between this person's perception of your gifts, and your own?

3. Ask God to begin to show you the gifts He has bestowed upon you.

4. Reread 1 Corinthians 12:8–11. What gifts do you earnestly desire? Seek for them by asking your heavenly Father.

15

POWERING UP YOUR CALL

This baptism of the Holy Ghost, this thing promised by the Father, this gift of power from on high, Christ expressly informed us is the indispensable condition of performing the work which He set before us.

Charles Finney, *Power from On High*

Spring 1992. McGregor Range, Fort Bliss, Texas. It is pitch black out here in the desert. The sky is blanketed with stars. My assistant and I are having the time of our lives. Our mission given by our battalion commander is to go out to each site where our 1-43 Patriot air defense artillery (1-43 ADA) missile units are located and see if we can test their secure perimeters with pyrotechnics.

We are loaded for bear, ready for anything! We possess the right ordnance for the mission—nothing lethal, but every kind of flare, noise maker, smoke grenade and star cluster in our unit's inventory stuffed in our vests and vehicle. We have sneaked up sight unseen and located a berm near the perimeter where we can hide and set off our fireworks. We fire up everything we have, light up the night sky and make the loudest racket possible.

Those on watch and guarding the perimeter open up with their machine guns, firing blanks and tracer rounds into the night sky in all directions, while we suppress our laughter at the thought of those soldiers not knowing who is out there, and why they are under attack. But before they send out patrols to search us out, we jump into our vehicle and head for the next night raid.

It is vital not only to load tanks and artillery with ammo, but to load the right kind of ammo for the right mission. Artillery units loading their tubes with illumination rounds, for example—rounds that simply light up the night sky, as my assistant and I used at Fort Bliss—will do little good if their objective is to destroy armored vehicles or a group of enemy soldiers.

Military might and power, along with strategy and diplomacy, are the foundations of winning wars. As we mentioned in our previous book *The Military Guide to Disarming Deception*, the acronym *DIME* is used for the kinds of power used by the U.S. It stands for the use of *diplomatic, informational, military* and *economic* tools as means of influence. When all options have been played out and the power of the military is brought to bear, this nation powers up the military by use of Presidential act and congressional approval. When that happens, the military loads up personnel, equipment, munitions and supplies and moves into battle array formations where needed.

It is the same for believers across the globe. You do not want to walk into a spiritually dark situation without the power of the Holy Spirit, the authority of the Word of God and the armor of God in place.

Now that you are finding your assignment and purpose in life, by the grace of God, what is next?

Stay Plugged In

Look at what happened to the disciples right after the powerful experience on the Mount of Transfiguration (which we discussed in chapter 7). After Jesus was transfigured into dazzling brightness and spoke with Moses and Elijah, Peter, James and John came down from that spiritual high with Jesus into a battle:

> When they came to the crowd, a man approached Jesus and knelt before him. "Lord, have mercy on my son," he said. "He has seizures and is suffering greatly. He often falls into the fire or into the water. I brought him to your disciples, but they could not heal him."
>
> "You unbelieving and perverse generation," Jesus replied, "how long shall I stay with you? How long shall I put up with you? Bring the boy here to me." Jesus rebuked the demon, and it came out of the boy, and he was healed at that moment.
>
> Then the disciples came to Jesus in private and asked, "Why couldn't we drive it out?"
>
> He replied, "Because you have so little faith. Truly I tell you, if you have faith as small as a mustard seed, you can say to this mountain, 'Move from here to there,' and it will move. Nothing will be impossible for you."
>
> Matthew 17:14–21

As the disciples in the valley below were battling demonic forces, the three on top of the mountain had been experiencing revival fire and the power of the Kingdom. But the fire experienced by Peter, James and John on the mountaintop probably faded as they made their way down into the valley below and joined the other disciples. Notice that their faith was tested immediately upon return to normalcy. When the disciples asked Jesus why they could not cast out the demon, He replied that their faith was not big enough.

201

Things look different on the mountain as opposed to in the valley. Remember each view. In this world no experience lasts forever. But it is vital to stay connected with the power source in both places. Colonel Peter Brzezinski explains:

> We've got to stay plugged in to God's power source, which the disciples did not understand. It was not about them; it was about having faith and trust in what God wanted to see done at the time for the people.
>
> It's the same in our day and age—it's not really about us. It's what the Lord wants to see done and letting Him use us for His purposes, for His honor and for His glory. The only way we get that kind of power is to stay in step with the Spirit by close fellowship with the Lord and His Word, living out those gifts He's given us, staying humble but staying plugged into God's power supply.
>
> You are loved and called to serve, but your life is not your own. You've been bought with a price; you belong to Him. So the life you live is really His life. Paul says, "I live by faith in the Son of God, who loved me and gave himself for me" (Galatians 2:20). That's where the power to accomplish the work in these challenging times comes from—when we stay plugged in.[1]

As revival spreads across the land, we must not let the fire die out through neglect. Many in revival experience the euphoria of excitement and joy, but that will soon fade as everyday life takes over, obstacles arise and Satan attacks. What we need to do is to stay plugged in through constant contact with the Holy Spirit and the Word of God.

Prayer Power

We have talked about one of the greatest U.S. Army generals in history, George S. Patton, a warrior unequaled in success on the battlefield in World War II. Why? According to Michael Keane, a Fellow of National Security at the Pacific Council on International Policy, here is Patton's philosophy:

> To be successful, Patton believed, a man must plan, work hard, and pray. A man prays to God for assistance in circumstances that he cannot foresee or control. Patton believed that without prayer, his soldiers would "crack up" under the unrelenting pressures of battle. Prayer does not have to take place in church but can be offered anywhere. Praying, he said, is "like plugging in on a current whose source is in Heaven." Prayer "completes the circuit. It is power."[2]

Let's look at one of the most dynamic battlefield prayers in the Bible, prayed by Joshua when he was confronting five Amorite kings in battle. Here is what happened:

> Joshua marched all night from Gilgal to Gibeon and made a surprise attack on the Amorite camp. The LORD made the enemy panic, and the Israelites started killing them right and left. They chased the Amorite troops up the road to Beth-Horon and kept on killing them. . . . The LORD made huge hailstones fall on them all the way to Azekah. More of the enemy soldiers died from the hail than from the Israelite weapons.
>
> The LORD was helping the Israelites defeat the Amorites that day. So about noon, Joshua prayed to the LORD loud enough for the Israelites to hear: "Our LORD, make the sun stop in the sky over Gibeon, and the moon stand still over Aijalon Valley." So the sun and the moon stopped and stood still until Israel defeated its enemies.
>
> Joshua 10:9–13 CEV

Talk about powering up! This is one of the most powerful and dynamic miracles in the entire Bible, so much so that the

Bible says in verse 14, "Never before and never since has the Lord done anything like that for someone who prayed. The LORD was really fighting for Israel." Imagine, the Lord agreed to stop and freeze the entire universe for a day.

The complexity of this miracle is so mind-boggling that most scientists and scholars assert that it did not actually happen. It could not have happened. It must have been figurative language, a poetic description, a mirage, an illusion, some sort of divine trickery. But no, according to the Bible, the sun did not move for a day in answer to Joshua's prayer.

Preparing for Our Mission

Why did God listen to a man and make the heavens stand still? There are at least three reasons, which we can apply to our own assignments.

Consistency

Joshua was consistent in following the commands of God. He did not veer off course; he stayed true to his calling.

God had told Joshua when he began leading the Israelites after Moses died:

"Be strong and very courageous. Be careful to obey all the law my servant Moses gave you; do not turn from it to the right or to the left, that you may be successful wherever you go. Keep this Book of the Law always on your lips; meditate on it day and night, so that you may be careful to do everything written in it. Then you will be prosperous and successful. Have I not commanded you? Be strong and courageous. Do not be afraid; do not be discouraged, for the Lord your God will be with you wherever you go."

Joshua 1:7–9

Joshua was focused.

The first thing we must do in preparing for our mission, then, is be consistent. Include Him in all your thinking and decisions. Consistency means holding on to the Lord every minute of every day.

Obedience

Second, when we obey the commands of God, we can expect His provision, support and favor.

After many military victories, the Bible says about Joshua:

> As the LORD commanded his servant Moses, so Moses commanded Joshua, and Joshua did it; he left nothing undone of all that the LORD commanded Moses.
>
> Joshua 11:15

Joshua, for sure, did not understand the entire plan of God for Israel, but one thing he did understand: When God directed, he obeyed. It is not for us to understand everything God has for our lives, but it is vitally important to carry out all that He leads us to accomplish.

Strength and Stamina

Third, notice that Joshua did all he could do so God could do all He could do! Joshua poured all he had into defeating the armies of the five Amorite kings.

The Amorites were trained warriors, descendants of Canaan and Ham (see Genesis 10:16). The prophet Amos described the Amorites as a mighty and formidable people of great height, "tall as the cedars and strong as the oaks" (Amos 2:9). Some theologians and scholars believe that the Amorites were actually giants, descended from the Rephaim, meaning "a terrible one" or "sons of the giant."[3] The Bible states that Og, an Amorite king of Bashan, was so big that "his bed was made of iron and was more than 13 feet long and 6 feet wide" (Deuteronomy 3:11 MSG).

So Joshua was not walking on easy street! He and his troops marched overnight from Gilgal to Gibeon, some twenty miles, then attacked when they arrived. A night march takes strength and speed, and to go right into battle takes considerable stamina. The army of Joshua needed God to show up, or they were not going to win this fight. Joshua needed and depended on a miracle. And he prayed aloud so all his troops could hear. He placed God's and his reputation on the line, and God came through.

The Battle for Souls

God told Joshua not to fear, and He is telling us not to fear. He is always working behind the scenes on our behalf, and He will always be with us. It may not be self-evident, but rest assured that, as Romans 8:31 says, "If God is for us, who can be against us?"

There will be times when we have done all we can do; we have reached our limit. That is when God takes over. He wants us to depend on Him and His strength, power, resources and provision. Just as God gave Joshua a mission that required him to depend on miraculous intervention for victory, so God takes great delight in our asking Him to intervene in our own battles.

"In this great last day's battle for souls," says prophecy expert Paul McGuire, believers in Christ must recognize that "God has sovereignly chosen to place us in these last days, for authentic revival before the Lord returns."[4]

Gospel music singer Mary Ann Peluso McGahan agrees:

God's mind right now is on the harvest—the last ingathering. It's time to find our mission in Christ and be obedient, and be a servant, with the harvest and eternity in mind. It is important for believers to know what their assignments are, how to do them and—number one—to know the Commander.[5]

STRATEGIC SPIRITUAL EXERCISES

1. Write down God's purpose and assignment for your life as you understand it today. How do you feel about it? Share it with a trusted friend or mentor.

2. Reread the story of the disciples' challenge in Matthew 17:14–21. Have you ever had a mountaintop experience, only for it to be shattered as you came back to your regular routine? What can you learn from this biblical account?

3. Read a chapter a day from Joshua 1–11 for the next eleven days, and see what difference it makes in your life.

4. How will you power up every day in the Holy Spirit, starting today?

16

USING THE GREATEST GIFT

Suffering persecution and aware of the signs of the times, an army of true Jesus followers will continue to arise like commandos. They will be part of an underground church that will be found preaching the return of Christ and the end of the age!

David Wilkerson, *The Vision and Beyond*

Spring 2018. San Antonio, Texas. I am nearing retirement from the U.S. Army after 32 years. I am in my small apartment in front of my computer, writing a manuscript called *The Making of a Warrior*. I am hoping that this manuscript will eventually become a published book. The topic is a nonprofit I have started in order to help veterans cope with life after war through hunting, fishing and other outdoor events. I am only a few pages into the manuscript when the Lord speaks to me.

How does He speak to me? My honest answer: I do not really know. Whether it is audible or just in my spirit remains a mystery. All I know is that the Lord and I have a conversation.

He impresses on me that I am headed in the wrong direction with the manuscript—that I need to start writing about His Second Coming, and that He wants me to prepare the Church and warn the world.

I say to the Lord, "Lord, nobody is really interested in reading about the end times and your Second Coming."

But He responds, *By the time this book is published, they will.*

The final published book became *The Military Guide to Armageddon*, published by Chosen Books on January 5, 2021. It quickly became a national bestseller. This was also the start of Battle Ready Ministries, dedicated to preparing the Church and warning the world about the Second Coming.

I have been asked several times during our Battle Ready Ministries conferences about love. How does love play into spiritual warfare, discipleship and our assignment from God? My response is always the same: Soldiers are trained in the basics of war because drill instructors want them not only to survive in combat, but to thrive as true warriors who know their craft. That is love!

Love is not the mushy, gushy, romantic tripe foisted on us by Hollywood and the media. Love is caring enough for people to give them the truth. According to 1 Corinthians 13, love is the greatest gift of all. The truth is, all believers are called in their assignments to love everyone enough to share the Gospel with them, and to come alongside fellow believers to encourage them in their faith journeys. In this chapter we will discover what biblical love is and how to use it in everyday life.

Divine love in the Greek is *agape,* meaning the love of God or Christ for humankind, or the unselfish love of one person for another without sexual implications. Love flows from the divine heart of God.[1]

Love is not something we conjure up or produce by an act of the will; it comes out of the heart of God into our innermost being. It is a God thing. Unfortunately, people get this type of love mixed up with the other types, such as a person's love for a spouse, or friendship love, or family love, even the love for country.

Agape love is action. John 3:16 states the ultimate divine action: "God so loved the world that he gave his one and only Son, that whoever believes in him shall not perish but have eternal life." The Greek word for "world" is *cosmos* or creation. God loved His creation so much that He sent Jesus to redeem it.

We must not forget, however, that God does not love the world's system—a system run by Satan that makes humanity the center of all things. James 4:4 admonishes us:

> You adulterous people, don't you know that friendship with the world means enmity against God? Therefore, anyone who chooses to be a friend of the world becomes an enemy of God.

God's Many-Sided Character

To take a deeper dive into unpacking love, let's look at the proverbial elephant in the room. One of the great sticking points for those outside the faith—and even for some inside—is the fact that God directed the children of Israel to kill all the Canaanites in the Promised Land:

> When the LORD your God brings you into the land you are entering to possess and drives out before you many nations—the Hittites, Girgashites, Amorites, Canaanites, Perizzites, Hivites and Jebusites, seven nations larger and stronger than you—and when the LORD your God has delivered them over to you and you have defeated them, then you must destroy them totally. Make no treaty with them, and show them no mercy.
>
> Deuteronomy 7:1–2

After the conquest of Jericho, for example: "They devoted the city to the LORD and destroyed with the sword every living thing in it—men and women, young and old, cattle, sheep and donkeys" (Joshua 6:21).

So the question is, How could a loving God have Israel destroy all the nations in Canaan and every living thing in Jericho? Even more, how could God destroy the whole planet and save only Noah and his family?

The twofold answer is the wickedness of the people being judged and the holiness of our God.

God had told Abraham, "In the fourth generation your descendants will come back here, for the sin of the Amorites has not yet reached its full measure" (Genesis 15:16). The Israelites would have to wait 430 years before the Amorites, indulging in not only idolatry but child sacrifice, were ripe for judgment.

Our holy and righteous God cannot permit sin. Heaven is filled only with those whose sins have been forgiven by Jesus Christ. Yes, God is love, but He is also a God of righteousness, holiness and judgment. Hence, the many-sided character of God.

Let's look at Jesus as the greatest example of what love looks like. He said in the Sermon on the Mount:

"Do not think that I have come to abolish the Law or the Prophets; I have not come to abolish them but to fulfill them. For truly I tell you, until heaven and earth disappear, not the smallest letter, not the least stroke of a pen, will by any means disappear from the Law until everything is accomplished.

"Therefore anyone who sets aside one of the least of these commands and teaches others accordingly will be called least in the kingdom of heaven, but whoever practices and teaches these commands will be called great in the kingdom of heaven.

For I tell you that unless your righteousness surpasses that of the Pharisees and the teachers of the law, you will certainly not enter the kingdom of heaven."

Matthew 5:17–20

Jesus was saying that the Law is still in effect and pointing out that our righteousness must surpass that of the Pharisees and teachers of the Law. How is this possible? What could He mean? That our own "righteousness" is not enough. We must have the righteousness of our heavenly Father conferred on us through faith in the shed blood of His Son, Jesus. Paul wrote, "In Christ Jesus you are all children of God through faith, for all of you who were baptized into Christ have clothed yourselves with Christ" (Galatians 3:26–27).

Well, then, what about love? Where does biblical love fit in here? The example of Jesus telling the truth in the Sermon on the Mount ("Unless your righteousness surpasses that of the Pharisees . . . you will certainly not enter the kingdom of heaven") is pure love. When any preacher or believer is not willing to tell you the truth about God, heaven, hell, the end times or anything else hard to hear, that is not love—it is pandering, trying to please at the expense of the truth.

The loving and caring Jesus who healed the sick, raised the dead, performed countless miracles and gave His life for the sins of the world is the same Jesus who confronted the religious leaders with their sin. He unleashed a verbal barrage of truth on them like no one else in history. Here are just three of what are called "the seven woes":

"Woe to you, teachers of the law and Pharisees, you hypocrites! You shut the door of the kingdom of heaven in people's faces. You yourselves do not enter, nor will you let those enter who are trying to.

213

"Woe to you, teachers of the law and Pharisees, you hypocrites! You travel over land and sea to win a single convert, and when you have succeeded, you make them twice as much a child of hell as you are.

"Woe to you, teachers of the law and Pharisees, you hypocrites! You are like whitewashed tombs, which look beautiful on the outside but on the inside are full of the bones of the dead and everything unclean. In the same way, on the outside you appear to people as righteous but on the inside you are full of hypocrisy and wickedness."

Matthew 23:13–15, 27–28

Jesus was at His unvarnished best in this passage. The targets of His message were furious enough to plot His death, and it is one of the reasons that, soon after, these very leaders had Jesus crucified. Yet if we look behind what Jesus was saying, we see grace rather than legalism. We see love. The Bible says that the Son of God "came from the Father, full of grace and truth" (John 1:14).

Pandering to legalism or hypocrisy has never led anyone to the truth of salvation. Many times confrontation is needed for love to penetrate the thick barrier of sin. In recent years the seeker-sensitive movement has discovered that catering to sinners only leads them to be comfortable in their sinful lifestyle. We do not recommend bashing people over the head with the Bible, but truth will win out in the end, even if people do not listen to it.

Telling the Hard Truth

Can you imagine if the Army practiced pandering to its soldiers? The results would be defeat on the battlefield. No, the Army, in its wisdom and many years of learning from history, tells the hard truth to those in basic training. They tell soldiers that life in combat will be brutal and dangerous. Only by training, discipline and real-world experience can they hope to survive war.

Is there any difference in the Church? People need to hear about faith, hope and love, but they also deserve to hear the unvarnished truth, the whole counsel of God.

I watched with amazement as actor Kelsey Grammer was interviewed by Kelly Ripa and Ryan Seacrest on their morning talk show. Grammer, discussing the movie *Jesus Revolution*, was in tears as he talked about portraying the late founder and senior pastor of Calvary Chapel Costa Mesa, Chuck Smith, who had helped start the Jesus people movement in Southern California, in the late 1960s and early '70s. I could see the love Kelsey had for Pastor Chuck, as well as Chuck's passion for the hippies. Real love is caring about the eternal destination of those around you.

Jesus replied to the question of one of the teachers of the Law about the greatest Commandment like this:

> "The most important one," answered Jesus, "is this: 'Hear, O Israel: The Lord our God, the Lord is one. Love the Lord your God with all your heart and with all your soul and with all your mind and with all your strength.' The second is this: 'Love your neighbor as yourself.' There is no commandment greater than these."
>
> Mark 12:29–31

Coco Perez, lead pastor of Horizon Church in West Sacramento, California, and a member of the Battle Ready Ministries board of directors, says about this reply of Jesus:

> Love was a huge part of the ministry of Jesus: Love God, love people. How we accomplish that mission in life is being filled

215

with the fruit of the Spirit (Galatians 5:22). The fruit of the Spirit is that supernatural strength that overcomes our natural weaknesses of hate, prejudice, gossip, slander and the works of the flesh.

Not the *power* of the Spirit, but the *fruit* of the Spirit. The apostle Paul in 1 Corinthians 12–14 makes a clear distinction between the two. You can have the gifts without the fruit and end up being "a noisy gong and a clanging cymbal." So instead of having the "anointing" of the Spirit, you become "annoying" of your own spirit!

Paul never apologized for chapter 13; he was only mirroring what Jesus said: "You will know them by their fruit" (Matthew 7:20 CEB). It is the fruit of the Spirit that changes us.[2]

Acts of Radical Love

Let's back up a bit, then. Yes, Jesus confronted the religious leaders of His day fearlessly. But let's not forget all the great acts of love He bestowed on His people: He healed the sick, raised the dead, released sinners from captivity, fed the five thousand, preached to starving souls, and many other things, culminating in His death for the sins of humankind.

So put God's love into action today. Find a hurting friend and give him or her your time, prayers and support. Pick up a neighbor who needs a ride to the doctor or to church. Invite a friend to your prayer meeting. Engage a skeptic in a dialogue about the truth in Christ. Allow the Holy Spirit to lead you to someone who needs Jesus.

=== STRATEGIC SPIRITUAL EXERCISES ===

1. Study the many facets of God and learn about how great our heavenly Father is.

2. Read 1 Corinthians 13 every day for a month and consider how Paul's description of *agape* love influences your day-to-day actions.

3. Think about the difference between pandering and love. What are ways you can move away from one and toward the other in your relations with those around you?

4. Put a list together of possible expressions of the radical love of Jesus.

CONCLUSION

In literature and in life we ultimately pursue, not conclusions, but beginnings.

Sam Tanenhaus, *Literature Unbound*

This is not the ending but just the beginning of your journey to find the purpose and assignment ordained by God for you.

Continue to press into God and His Word. You will encounter obstacles, times of frustration and just the plain, ordinary things of life to contend with. And be sure to understand what the great basketball coach John Wooden once said: "Don't mistake activity with achievement."[1] Sometimes we need to stop the activity and be quiet before God to understand His purpose for our lives.

All of us get caught up in the busyness of life, thinking that is just the way it must be, but nothing is further from the truth. As Coach Wooden said, we must not equate busyness with success. God has instilled in all mankind the desire for greatness, to excel, to fulfill our destiny and purpose. Many people run around thinking that the busier they are, the more important and successful they are. But ask yourself, What is my main goal in life? What is my ultimate aim? In other words, take the long view. The most important thing to remember and focus on is not the temporal but the eternal. Maintain an eternal perspective.

Many who have lost loved ones in untimely deaths ask God why. There are many difficult situations in life that seemingly make no sense and to which there are no answers. If we take the temporal view—the view that is shortsighted, only for the now—we will always come up short.

But God lives in all dimensions and outside of time, in the eternal past as well as the infinite future as well as the ever-present now: "Jesus Christ is the same yesterday and today and forever" (Hebrews 13:8). And Revelation 1:8: "'I am the Alpha and the Omega,' says the Lord God, 'who is, and who was, and who is to come, the Almighty.'" And Isaiah 57:15: "This is what the high and exalted One says—he who lives forever, whose name is holy."

We must, at the end of the day, trust God for all situations in life, especially when we do not understand the current situation, whatever it may be. We will not understand many things in this life, this side of eternity. But all things will be revealed in the life to come. There are leaders who seemingly get away with corruption now, but we must remember that there is a Great White Throne Judgment to come:

Then I saw a great white throne and him who was seated on it. The earth and the heavens fled from his presence, and there was no place for them. And I saw the dead, great and small, standing before the throne, and books were opened. Another book was opened, which is the book of life. The dead were judged according to what they had done as recorded in the books. The sea gave up the dead that were in it, and death and Hades gave up the dead that were in them, and each person was judged according to what they had done. Then death and Hades were thrown into the lake of fire. The lake of fire is the second death. Anyone whose name was not found written in the book of life was thrown into the lake of fire.

Revelation 20:11–15

Our eternal destiny, then, must always be at the forefront of our minds and the center of our hearts. When we consider our assignment and purpose for today, nothing is more important than our eternal destiny. So it was with the heroes of the faith:

All these people were still living by faith when they died. They did not receive the things promised; they only saw them and welcomed them from a distance, admitting that they were for-eigners and strangers on earth. People who say such things show that they are looking for a country of their own. If they had been thinking of the country they had left, they would have had opportunity to return. Instead, they were longing for a better country—a heavenly one. Therefore God is not ashamed to be called their God, for he has prepared a city for them.

Hebrews 11:13–16

The heroes of the faith—including Enoch, Abraham and others we have talked about in this book—were not short-sighted; they had the eternal view in mind. Think about it: This life at best may last eighty to ninety years, but eternity lasts forever. The physical life God has granted us is just a prelude to eternity—but vitally important since in it we choose our eternal destination, either heaven or hell.

Most believers, although they spend hours or even months planning a vacation, do not fully understand heaven and their final destination. It is important to understand that when we

221

die in this life, we go to the "intermediate heaven" to be with Jesus, our loved ones, and the hosts of heaven. But that is not our final destination. Believe it or not, our final destination is on the renewed earth with Jesus, reigning in the New Jerusalem. Look at Revelation 21:1–4:

> Then I saw "a new heaven and a new earth," for the first heaven and the first earth had passed away, and there was no longer any sea. I saw the Holy City, the new Jerusalem, coming down out of heaven from God, prepared as a bride beautifully dressed for her husband. And I heard a loud voice from the throne saying, "Look! God's dwelling place is now among the people, and he will dwell with them. They will be his people, and God himself will be with them and be their God. He will wipe every tear from their eyes. There will be no more death or mourning or crying or pain, for the old order of things has passed away."

You see, when God created the earth, it was meant to last forever. Then the Fall of mankind happened, and the earth was marred with sin and death. But God sent Jesus to redeem not only humankind, but the entire cosmos, including planet earth. The earth, in the final analysis, will be completely redeemed and renovated. As John wrote, "Then I saw 'a new heaven and a new earth,' for the first heaven and the first earth had passed away" (Revelation 21:1).

This life is not the end, then, but only the beginning of all eternity. Please choose Jesus and eternal life in heaven with Him. We hope to see you there.

ACKNOWLEDGMENTS

As always, God gets all the glory for His purpose being fulfilled in this book.

Along with Him, I, Colonel David J. Giammona, wish to acknowledge my beautiful wife, Esther, for her inspiration to write this book, along with all my adult children: Micah, Catarina, Melissa and their wonderful spouses, Andrea, Andrew and Luis. To my great co-author, Troy Anderson, and the whole Battle Ready Ministries team: Irene Anderson, John Barker, Colonel (retired) Pete Brzezinski, Kevin Callahan, Major General (retired) Robert Dees, Jim Ellis, the Reverend Kevin Jessip, Colonel (retired) Scott McChrystal, Chris McGahan, Mary Ann McGahan, Jerry Moses and Pastor Coco Perez.

We would further like to thank those who graciously took time to do interviews for the book, including Lieutenant General William G. "Jerry" Boykin, Colonel Brzezinski, Colonel McChrystal, Mary Ann Peluso McGahan, Paul McGuire, Eric Metaxas, Troy Miller, Alex Newman, Pastor Coco Perez, Pastor Paul Pickern, Pastor Todd Smith and Kevin Sorbo.

In addition, we would like to thank everyone who agreed to endorse the book, including Pastor Jimmy Evans, Dr. Robert

Jeffress, Rabbi Jonathan Bernis, Kevin Sorbo, Todd Starnes, Chris Salcedo, Major General Bob Dees and Cynthia Garrett.

I, Troy Anderson, would like to thank our Bible study group in Irvine, California, led by David and Esther, who have prayed for the Lord's guidance and blessings over this project and others for more than a decade. I would also like to thank Jerry Moses, assistant to the president at Movieguide, for his wisdom, prayers and belief in this project.

We would also like to thank our ingenious literary agent, Bryan Norman, CEO and president of Alive Literary Agency, for his encouragement and belief in this series of books.

Finally, we would like to thank our incredible team at Chosen Books, including Jane Campbell, former Chosen Books editorial director, who edited our previous books and agreed to edit this one as well; senior acquisitions editor David Sluka; marketing manager Stephanie Smith; publicist Rebecca Schriner; marketing and publicity associate Bria Conway; and senior editor Natasha Sperling.

May the Holy Spirit use *Your Mission in God's Army* to inspire millions of people to join Adonai's army, discover their God-given destinies, and help bring in the end-times harvest. As Jesus said to His disciples, "The harvest truly is plentiful, but the laborers are few. Therefore pray the Lord of the harvest to send out laborers into His harvest" (Matthew 9:37–38 NKJV).

NOTES

Preface

1. Aaron Earls, "Vast Majority of Pastors See Signs of End Times in Current Events," Lifeway Research, April 7, 2020, https://research.lifeway.com/2020/04/07/vast-majority-of-pastors-see-signs-of-end-times-in-current-events.

2. Jeff Diamant, "About Four-in-Ten US Adults Believe Humanity Is 'Living in the End Times,'" Pew Research Center, December 8, 2022, https://www.pewresearch.org/fact-tank/2022/12/08/about-four-in-ten-u-s-adults-believe-humanity-is-living-in-the-end-times.

Introduction

1. *Discovery Bible* (2021), s.v. "aiốnios," HELPS Word-studies, https://biblehub.com/greek/166.htm.

2. Leah Collins, "Job Unhappiness Is at a Staggering All-Time High, According to Gallup," CNBC, August 12 , 2022, https://www.cnbc.com/2022/08/12/job-unhappiness-is-at-a-staggering-all-time-high-according-to-gallup.html.

Chapter 1 What Is Your Assignment?

1. *Cambridge Dictionary*, s.v. "mission," https://dictionary.cambridge.org/us/dictionary/english/mission.

2. *Cambridge Dictionary*, s.v. "assignment," https://dictionary.cambridge.org/us/dictionary/english/assignment.

3. Walter A. Elwell, *Baker's Evangelical Dictionary of Biblical Theology* (Grand Rapids: Baker Books, 1996), s.v. "mission," https://www.biblestudytools.com/dictionaries/bakers-evangelical-dictionary/mission.html.

4. Kevin Sorbo, January 3, 2023, Zoom interview with Troy Anderson.

5. Sorbo, interview.

6. Sorbo, interview.

7. Sorbo, interview.

8. Sorbo, interview.

9. John H. Sammis, "Trust and Obey," 1887, public domain.

Chapter 2 Preparing for Your Mission

1. Msgr. James H. O'Neill, "The True Story of the Patton Prayer," *The New American*, January 12, 2004, https://www.fpparchive.org/media/documents/us_military/The%20True%20Story%20of%20the%20Patton%20Prayer_Msgr.%20James%20H.%20O'Neill_January%2012,%202004_The%20New%20American.pdf.

2. Keith Speights, "What Percentage of Businesses Fail in Their First Year?," Fox Business, May 3, 2017, https://www.foxbusiness.com/markets/what-percentage-of-businesses-fail-in-their-first-year.

3. Todd Smith, January 13, 2023, Zoom interview with Col. David J. Giammona and Troy Anderson.

4. Richard Wurmbrand, *Tortured for Christ* (Bartlesville, Okla.: Living Sacrifice Book Company, 1967), 150.

5. Smith, interview.

6. Aaron Earls, "Vast Majority of Pastors See Signs of End Times in Current Events," Lifeway Research, April 20, 2020, https://research.lifeway.com/2020/04/07/vast-majority-of-pastors-see-signs-of-end-times-in-current-events.

7. "'I Didn't Do Anything, It Was God Who Made Me Play Like This,' Says Soccer Star Lionel Messi," Bibliatodo News, October 11, 2021, https://www.bibliatodo.com/En/christian-news/i-didnt-do-anything-it-was-god-who-made-me-play-like-this-says-soccer-star-lionel-messi.

8. Adrian Rogers, "Faith in Jesus . . . Not Faith in Faith," Love Worth Finding with Adrian Rogers, April 20, 2017, https://www.lwf.org/daily-devotions/faith-in-jesus-not-faith-in-faith.

Chapter 3 Sacred vs. Secular

1. *Cambridge Dictionary*, s.v. "reason," https://dictionary.cambridge.org/us/dictionary/english/reason.

2. Hugh Whelchel, "When Will the Church Overcome the Sacred-Secular Divide?," Institute for Faith, Work & Economics, December 8, 2016, https://tifwe.org/overcoming-the-sacred-secular-divide.

3. *Seinfeld*, season 5, episode 22, "The Opposite," written by Larry David, Jerry Seinfeld, and Andy Cowan, directed by Tom Cherones, aired May 19, 1994, https://www.imdb.com/title/tt0697744/characters/nm0004517.

4. Tim Irwin, Ph.D., *Derailed: Five Lessons Learned from Catastrophic Failures of Leadership* (Nashville: Thomas Nelson, 2009).

Chapter 4 The DNA Factor

1. *Cambridge Dictionary*, s.v. "DNA," https://dictionary.cambridge.org
/us/dictionary/english/dna?q=DNA.

2. Stacy Sampson and Jill Seladi-Schulman, "DNA Explained and Explored," Healthline, February 11, 2022, https://www.healthline.com/health
/what-is-dna#takeaway.

3. Alex Newman, *The New American*, "About the *New American* Magazine," https://thenewamerican.com/about.

4. Alex Newman, January 26, 2023, Zoom interview with Col. David J.
Giammona and Troy Anderson.

5. Newman, interview.

6. Rev. Todd Smith, January 13, 2023, Zoom interview with Col. David
J. Giammona and Troy Anderson.

7. "The Assyrians," Bible History, accessed September 22, 2023, https://
bible-history.com/old-testament/the-assyrians.

Chapter 5 The World's System

1. Hugh Ross, *Why the Universe Is the Way It Is* (Grand Rapids: Baker,
2008), 35.

2. "The Matrix Plot," Internet Movie Database, accessed September 22,
2023, https://www.imdb.com/title/tt0133093/plotsummary.

3. Eric Metaxas, February 10, 2023, Zoom interview with Col. David J.
Giammona and Troy Anderson.

4. Metaxas, interview.

5. Jim Rohn, *Challenge to Succeed: A Philosophy for Successful Living*
(audio CD, January 1, 1991).

Chapter 6 Living Out Faith in the Real World

1. "Pointe du Hoc Ranger Monument," American Battle Monuments
Commission, last updated April 5, 2023, https://api.abmc.gov/Pointe-du-Hoc.

2. "Pointe du Hoc Ranger Monument."

3. Daniel R. Champagne, "The Pointe du Hoc Rangers: A Madman's
D-Day Mission," Warfare History Network, https://warfarehistorynetwork
.com/the-pointe-du-hoc-rangers-a-madmans-d-day-mission.

4. "Pointe du Hoc Ranger Monument."

5. Champagne, "The Pointe du Hoc Rangers."

6. William Carey, *The Journal and Selected Letters of William Carey*
(Macon, Ga.: Smyth & Helwys, 2022), 52.

7. Nathan A. Finn, "Missionaries You Should Know: William Carey,"
International Mission Board, July 31, 2018, https://www.imb.org/2018/07
/31/missionaries-you-should-know-william-carey/.

8. Alex Newman, January 26, 2023, Zoom interview with Col. David J.
Giammona and Troy Anderson.

9. Newman, interview.

10. "Jim Elliot: Story and Legacy," Christianity.com, June 5, 2020, https://www.christianity.com/church/church-history/timeline/1901-2000/jim-elliot-no-fool-11634862.html.

11. Eric Metaxas, February 10, 2023, Zoom interview with Col. David J. Giammona and Troy Anderson.

Chapter 7 Developing Your Faith

1. Rick Warren, *Created to Dream: The 6 Phases God Uses to Grow Your Faith* (Grand Rapids: Zondervan, 2023), 7–8.

2. Col. Scott McChrystal, March 2, 2023, Zoom interview with Troy Anderson.

3. Eric Metaxas, February 10, 2023, Zoom interview with Col. David J. Giammona and Troy Anderson.

4. William Gurnall, *The Christian in Complete Armour* (Lindale, Tex.: World Challenge, Inc., David Wilkerson Crusades, 1988), 27.

5. Kali Martin, "Private First Class Desmond Thomas Doss Medal of Honor," The National World War II Museum, October 12, 2020, https://www.nationalww2museum.org/war/articles/private-first-class-desmond-thomas-doss-medal-of-honor.

6. Martin, "Private First Class Desmond Thomas Doss."

Chapter 8 Plans and Purpose

1. William Pietersen, "Von Clausewitz on War: Six Lessons for the Modern Strategist," Columbia Business School, February 12, 2016, https://business.columbia.edu/cgi-strategy/chazen-global-insights/von-clausewitz-war-six-lessons-modern-strategist.

2. "Overweight and Obesity Statistics," National Institute of Diabetes and Digestive and Kidney Diseases, National Institutes of Health, last reviewed September 2021, https://www.niddk.nih.gov/health-information/health-statistics/overweight-obesity.

3. Sara, "I Spy a Fad Diet! Your Guide to Critically Evaluating Diet and Wellness Trends," Kendall Reagan Nutrition Center, Colorado State University, June 2023, https://www.chhs.colostate.edu/krnc/monthly-blog/i-spy-a-fad-diet-your-guide-to-critically-evaluating-diet-and-wellness-trends/.

4. Charles Finney, *Power from On High* (Fort Washington, Pa.: CLC, 2022), 17.

Chapter 9 Faith and Friction

1. Alex Lovelace, *Encyclopaedia Britannica*, s.v. "George Patton," https://www.britannica.com/biography/George-Smith-Patton.

2. Lovelace, "George Patton."

3. Carl von Clausewitz, *Vom Kriege (On War)*, book 1, chapter 7, "Friction in War," https://www.clausewitz.com/readings/OnWar1873/BK1ch07.html.

4. Eric Metaxas, February 10, 2023, Zoom interview with Col. David J. Giammona and Troy Anderson.

5. Metaxas, interview.

6. Metaxas, interview.

7. Mary Ann Peluso McGahan, March 14, 2023, Zoom interview with Troy Anderson.

8. McGahan, interview.

9. Rick Warren, *Created to Dream: The 6 Phases God Uses to Grow Your Faith* (Grand Rapids: Zondervan, 2023), 57.

10. Trevor Freeze, "Franklin Graham: 'Every Demon in Hell Has Been Turned Loose,'" *Charisma*, May 23, 2023, https://mycharisma.com/spiritled -living/franklin-graham-every-demon-in-hell-has-been-turned-loose.

Chapter 10 A New Purpose

1. "The Twentieth Maine," National Guard, accessed September 22, 2023, https://www.nationalguard.mil/Resources/Image-Gallery/Historical-Paint ings/Heritage-Series/Twentieth-Maine/.

2. Garry E. Adelman, *The Myth of Little Round Top* (Gettysburg, Pa.: Thomas Publications, 2003), 61–62.

3. Col. Peter Brzezinski, March 16, 2023, Zoom interview with Troy Anderson.

4. Brzezinski, interview.

5. Brzezinski, interview.

6. Paul Pickern, March 13, 2023, Zoom interview with Troy Anderson.

7. Pickern, interview.

8. Pickern, interview.

Chapter 11 Growing in Faith and Your Assignment

1. Martin Kelly, "5 Key Causes of World War I," ThoughtCo.com, updated March 26, 2020, https://www.thoughtco.com/causes-that-led-to-world-war -i-105515#.

2. *Encyclopaedia Britannica*, s.v. "Pharisee," https://www.britannica.com /topic/Pharisee.

3. "Who Were the Pharisees in the Bible?," Christianity.com, July 27, 2010, https://www.christianity.com/jesus/birth-of-jesus/genealogy-and-jewish -heritage/how-were-the-pharisees-legalistic.html.

4. Steve Warren, "Anne Graham Lotz: This Could Be the 'Last Great Awak-ening' as Asbury Revival Fires Reach New Campuses," CBN, February 22, 2023, https://www1.cbn.com/cbnnews/us/2023/february/anne-graham-lotz-this -could-be-the-last-great-awakening-as-asbury-revival-fires-reach-new-campuses.

5. Mary Ann Peluso McGahan, March 14, 2023, Zoom interview with Troy Anderson.

6. McGahan, interview.

7. McGahan, interview.

Chapter 12 A True Follower of Christ

1. "Aubrey S. Newman, 90, Colonel Famed for 'Follow Me' Battle Cry," *New York Times*, January 22, 1994, https://www.nytimes.com/1994/01/22/obituaries/aubrey-s-newman-90-colonel-famed-for-follow-me-battle-cry.html.

2. *Strong's Concordance*, s.v. "archón," https://biblehub.com/greek/758.htm.

3. Tim Lott, "Jordan Peterson: 'The Pursuit of Happiness Is a Pointless Goal,'" *Guardian*, January 21, 2018, https://www.theguardian.com/global/2018/jan/21/jordan-peterson-self-help-author-12-steps-interview.

4. Holly Bieler, "Meet Shen Schulz, Luxury Real Estate Agent Born and Raised in Malibu," *Malibu Magazine*, January 28, 2020, https://www.malibumag.com/community/meet-shen-schulz-luxury-real-estate-agent-born-and-raised-in-malibu.

5. Andrew Knighton, "Front-Line General—Norman Cota in WWII," War History Online, August 31, 2018, https://www.warhistoryonline.com/world-war-ii/general-norman-cota.html.

6. Troy Miller, March 10, 2023, Zoom interview with Col. David J. Giammona and Troy Anderson.

Chapter 13 The Commander of the Heavenly Host

1. Col. Peter Brzezinski, March 16, 2023, Zoom interview with Troy Anderson.

2. Lieut. Gen. William G. "Jerry" Boykin, March 17, 2023, Zoom interview with Col. David J. Giammona, Troy Anderson and Pastor Coco Perez.

3. Paul McGuire, March 24, 2023, Zoom interview with Col. David J. Giammona and Troy Anderson.

4. McGuire, interview.

5. Bryant G. Wood, "The Walls of Jericho," Associates for Biblical Research, June 9, 2008, https://biblearchaeology.org/research/conquest-of-canaan/3625-the-walls-of-jericho.

6. Brzezinski, interview.

Chapter 14 Your Assignment and Your Gifts

1. Col. Scott McChrystal, March 2, 2023, Zoom interview with Troy Anderson.

2. Col. Peter Brzezinski, March 16, 2023, Zoom interview with Troy Anderson.

3. Brzezinski, interview.

Chapter 15 Powering Up Your Call

1. Col. Peter Brzezinski, March 16, 2023, Zoom interview with Troy Anderson.

2. Michael Keane, "The Religious Life of George S. Patton," Historyon theNet.com, accessed September 22, 2023, https://www.historyonthenet.com /the-religious-life-of-george-s-patton.

3. H. Porter, *International Standard Bible Encyclopedia*, James Orr, ed. (1915), s.v. "rephaim," https://www.biblestudytools.com/encyclopedias/isbe /rephaim.html.

4. Paul McGuire, March 24, 2023, Zoom interview with Col. David J. Giammona and Troy Anderson.

5. Mary Ann Peluso McGahan, March 14, 2023, Zoom interview with Troy Anderson.

Chapter 16 Using the Greatest Gift

1. Dictionary.com, s.v. "agape," https://www.dictionary.com/browse /agape.

2. Pastor Coco Perez, March 28, 2023, email interview with Troy Anderson.

Conclusion

1. John Wooden, *Coach Wooden's Leadership Game Plan for Success* (New York: McGraw-Hill, 2009), 133.

U.S. Army chaplain (Colonel) David J. Giammona is an end-times expert, scholar, bestselling author, speaker, and president and CEO of Battle Ready Ministries. He retired in 2018 after 32 years of miltiary service in the United States Army. He is co-author of the national bestsellers *The Military Guide to Armageddon* and *The Military Guide to Disarming Deception*. He and his wife, Esther, live at their home on the 46-acre Warrior Refuge near Columbus, Georgia. Find out more at DavidJ Giammona.com and Battle-Ready.org.

Troy Anderson is a Pulitzer Prize–nominated investigative journalist, bestselling author, vice president and COO of Battle Ready Ministries, president of the Inspire Literary Group, executive editor of The Return International and founder of Prophecy Investigators. During his three-decade career in journalism, he has worked as a reporter, bureau chief and editorial writer at *The Los Angeles Daily News*, *The Press-Enterprise* and other newspapers, and he served as executive editor of *Charisma* magazine and Charisma Media. He is co-author of the national bestsellers *The Babylon Code, Trumpocalypse, The Military Guide to Armageddon* and *The Military Guide to Disarming Deception*. He and his family live in Irvine, California. Find out more at TroyAnderson.us, Battle-Ready.org, InspireLiterary.com and ProphecyInvestigators.org.

PERSONAL NOTES